NOBODY:

ME AT AGE 40:
I'm A Virgin…

Embracing Your Life's Journey

Frenda Rodgers

DEDICATION

I would like to dedicate this book to my mother, Arnater Rodgers and my father, Fernando Timberlake. My love for you both is and will forever be unconditional. I love you both forever!

My sisters, Marquitta, Victoria and Danyil, I cannot imagine life without either of you. Sisters are gifts from God, and I thank God for each of you every day. As long as I got the three of you, I am good for life. I love you ladies to the moon and back!

My sisters, Topeka, Alexis, Britney and Whitney & brothers, Michael (RIP), Malvin and Akilo I love each of you beyond words. Although we did not grow up together as sibling should, I thank God every day for bringing us back together. We are now forever connected.

To my 12 beautiful and amazing godchildren: Jymirah Mone Maxine, Geoffrey III, Josiah Nathan, Kristopher O'Neil, Naila Marai, Mya Nicole, Micah Ya'vor, Brooke Samantha, Karis Sarai, Krystal Rose, Mylo Jacob & Jackson Alexander William I thank God for each of you! You all make life worth living!

To my sister-chicks (RIP Valencia), sister-friends, sister-cousins, Spelman sisters, ANWA sisters, SF sisters and sistas; I thank each of you for loving me simply for me! Thanks for helping me show the world, women can do get along. I love you ladies forever!

I want to thank my spiritual parents Dr. Matthew L. Stevenson III and Apostle Kamilah Stevenson for all of your love, support, encouragement and investments. I have the dopest Pops & Momz in the world! I love you both beyond measure!

Lastly, I would like to dedicate this book to in memories of my great-grandparents; Tommie & Estella Rodgers; my cousins, Marcea Rodgers, Carmenda Woodard, Cleon Wilson & Deonte Milner and my uncle, Tommie Lee Rodgers.

TABLE OF CONTENTS

ACKNOWLEDGMENTS

I would like to acknowledge the many mentors who have richly blessed my life in more ways than I can count. I have been blessed with so many women who have taken the time to train, teach, disciple, mentor and invest in my life. I honor, appreciate and love each of you. Thanks Dr. Latunja O. Williams, Dr. Venisa Green, Ms. Regina Y. Huston, Ms. LeeAndra Khan, Apostle Mary-Alice Isleib, Dr. Marlene Carson, Mrs. LaTia Vaughan and Apostle Nina Marie Leslie (RIP).

INTRODUCTION

Life is a journey. Throughout this journey, we will learn lessons, encounter hardships, celebrate victories, overcome obstacles, experience joys and highs as well as suffer grief and loss. Our journey ultimately leads us to our purpose, the thing we were born to do, be, and manifest. Through story-telling, comic relief, positive affirmations and mental health tips; I share my life struggles, failures, triumphs, victories and lessons that taught me how to accept and embrace my life's journey. I would like to welcome each of you to the story of my journey.

CHAPTER 1: MY BIRTHDAY

One of my earliest memories was a time I was sitting on a couch, I believe, with two of my cousins. I cannot remember exactly which cousins; I think they were younger than me, though. We were sitting on a couch in the living room watching maybe 10 or 15 other children play at what looked like at a party. I know it was a party because there were party hats, party decorations, balloons, and kids were running around and having a good time. I remember seeing a cake, and maybe food or snacks.

I remember sitting on the couch, but the crazy part is, I don't remember talking. Honestly, I don't know how old I was. I am thinking I may have been about two years old. The couch was beige, and it had plastic on it. It was in the living room and the floor was hardwood. Looking back at old pictures, I know the kids playing at the party were my cousins. I remember my older cousins Marc and Mane-Mane coming by the couch from time to time to check on me. They were like five or six, but I remember them coming to the couch trying to give me party favors and snacks. When I think about my cousin Marc, I always think about how he has always looked out for me. He was like the big brother that I never had. I remember him coming to the couch and asking, "You okay, you okay?"

Another thing that I remember was, being content with sitting on that sofa while all the other kids ran around and played. I don't remember having a desire to even get off the couch. As I look back and think about my earliest memory, some things stick out to me. I think it was my second birthday. The party was for me. I remember being given a lot of attention from both the kids and the adults in the house, especially my mommy, who seemed to be running back and forth but occasionally stopping to kiss me or fix my hair and clothes. I know it sounds crazy, but I remember all those details.

As stated before, I seemed to be content with sitting on that couch while all the other kids played. I have always had this memory in the back of my mind. There were times when I was not sure if I made the whole thing up. However, I realized that this memory could possibly be legit when my mom told me that I did not learn how to walk until after I turned age two. I was home from college on a break. My mom and I were watching a movie or TV show and somehow we got on the subject of what's the average age a baby learns to walk. My mom made a comment like, "The average age is probably a year old, but girl you did not learn to walk until you were well over two years old!" She chuckled. I responded surprised and confused, "What???? How??? Why???" My mom laughed even harder. "What do you mean what, how and why? Girl, you were so scary! I guess you were afraid of falling. We (meaning her and my great-grandmother-Mama) tried everything to get you to walk. Then one day, I got tired of carrying two babies around (my sister and I are 18 months apart) and I stopped picking you up and carrying you around. You cried, but slowly and surely you started standing up and holding on to things to get around. Before I knew it, you were walking. I remember the first time you took steps, I was in shock. You just started walking on your own one day."

I don't know at what age most people can recall their earliest memory. I have heard a few people say the earliest age they could remember was maybe three or four. Others say five or six. It's rare to hear people say they remember as early as two years old. This is why I was not sure if this memory was valid. After getting over the shock of not being able to walk until age two, I asked my mom if I had a party when I was a baby. She verified that I did have a birthday party at my great-grandmother's apartment right off of Hamlin. She said my sister, Marquitta, was about six months and she was trying to host my birthday party while carrying around two babies because I still could not walk. So she sat me on the couch, and that is where I remained for the duration of my party.

I was born during the blizzard of 1979 in Chicago. I remember having a birthday party when I was about eight at Showbiz Pizza, currently known as Chuck E. Cheese. I remember this particular party because it was snowing really hard. I remember being scared that we would get snowed in at my party. I was born and raised in Chicago. I was familiar with snow, but I remember being afraid for some reason. I remember my mom looking back at me in the car and asking me if I was excited about my party. She took one look at my face and knew something was wrong. I remember my mom saying, "Girl, don't worry about this snow. People drive in this kind of weather all of the time. People are going to come to your party." I wasn't worried about whether people were going to come to my party or not; I was so scared about what the outside would look like once my party was over. I remember my mom saying something like, "Girl, this is nothing. You were born during that massive blizzard of 1979, now that was scary."

We got to my party and I enjoyed myself, but I kept thinking, "What is the outside going to look like once we leave? Will we be able to get back home?" I don't know, at age eight, I don't understand why my mind worked that way, but it did. I had anxiety and worried about everything. I remember as a young child, not being able to sleep at night due to fear and anxiety. I worried about something as small as did I complete my homework assignment correctly or something as big as fearing someone would break into our house to hurt us. I worried about everything.

I recently researched the blizzard of 1979. I don't know why but I research random events that occurred the year I was born. According to my research, it snowed from January 13th to January 15th nonstop; there was like 21 inches of snow. The blizzard was so bad, there were even deaths, I believe five people died, and 15 were seriously injured. One of the most significant issues with that blizzard was the fact that the mayor at the time, Michael Bilandic, did not strategically deploy snowplows in time. Snow remained on the ground until like March. The blizzard affected travel, especially for those who used public transportation, CTA buses, and the trains (L-system). What should have been a 15-minute bus ride or train ride, took several hours. I often think about what it was like for a pregnant 19-year-old, first-time mother to get herself to the hospital while dealing with issues of transportation and mounts of snow everywhere. My mother was 18 when she got pregnant with me; she graduated from high school that May and turned 19 that November. Then she gave birth to me in January of that next year.

Another thing that I found out about the year I was born was due to the mishandling of the blizzard Mayor Bilandic lost to Jane Byrd for the mayoral race. Jane Byrd became the first female mayor of Chicago in 1979. I thought it was interesting that I was born in 1979 when the first female mayor of Chicago was elected. Here I am, 40 years later, and the first African-American female mayor, Lori Lightfoot was recently elected.

LIFE/MENTAL HEALTH TIP(S):

Your life is significant. The day, year, place, and era you were born in are all specific and important. You were born on purpose (it does not matter what the circumstances were behind how you got here) and with a purpose. Never take yourself or your life for granted.

Jeremiah 1:5 (NLV)

Before I formed you in the womb I knew you, before you were born I set you apart; I appointed you as a prophet to the nations.

CHAPTER 2: MY NAME

I was blessed to attend one of the best historically black colleges and universities in the world, Spelman College. I'll talk a little bit more in detail about my experience getting to Spelman and life at Spelman later in a later chapter. I remember an assignment from my English 101 class, and honestly, I struggled with English and grammar. I didn't know how bad I struggled with writing and sometimes speaking, until I got to college. Spelman College is a private, liberal arts, women's college in Atlanta, GA. I attended college with young ladies who looked like me. However, our elementary and high school educational experiences were vastly different.

Some of these ladies attended boarding school; some attended private high schools and paid tuition, some were homeschooled, some lived in communities in which education was both valued and funded while others attended public schools where resources, funding and rigor are based on the racially, socially and economically inequitable neighborhoods in which the schools reside. I am one of the others. I tell everyone, I got into Spelman by God's grace. I had a fantastic English professor. She saw my struggle, she saw my effort and she did not judge me. She would say, "You're a good storyteller, I get what you're trying to say," but my grammar was off. I didn't know where to put commas; I didn't know where to start a new main idea. I am 18 years old, a high school graduate, actually valedictorian of my high school, and I was still struggling with elementary level grammar.

We were given an assignment to write a paper about the meaning of our name. I remember thinking, "I do not know how I am going to write a whole paper on my name. My mom made it up!" As a kid, I hated my name. I remember in second grade I would change my name on my papers to Brenda with a "B." Because my name was different, people made fun of me for it. My name made me stand out and I just wanted a "normal" name like Brittany, Mary or Nicole. I remember changing the "F" to a "B" on all my papers. My teacher wrote a note on one of my papers stating, "Stop writing this on your papers, this is not your name. Your name is Frenda, it's not Brenda, and if you do it again, I'm not going to grade your paper." When I read that my teacher would no longer grade my assignments I worked so hard on, I immediately changed my name right back to Frenda. I was always competitive in school. I wanted to have all A's. I wanted to be perfect.

The assignment was to explain the meaning of your name; why did your parents give you your name, and how does your name represent your family? I sat there staring at the assignment filled with anxiety. I was trying to figure out how I was going to type a paper on the meaning of a made up name. The family representation part was a whole other issue. I had my mother's maiden name but I still lacked a lot of knowledge about my mother's family history. Her mother, my grandmother passed when my mom was 12 years old. Although her father was around, she and her siblings were raised by her grandparents on her father's side. I knew all of my aunts, uncle and immediate cousins. I knew nothing about my extended family. I was beyond overwhelmed.

One of my Spelman sisters, who is one of my best friends today, Kendrea was also in that English 101 class. Kendrea and I lived in the same dorm. Her room was next door. Kendrea was so smart she could write a paper the night before it was due. I, on the hand, had to start writing my papers at least a week in advance and go through two more drafts to end of with the final product. I remember slowly walking to Kendrea's room. She was my friend but I was embarrassed at the fact that school was not coming easy for me. However, if anyone could encourage and motivate me to keep working harder it was Kendrea. When I mentioned the assignment, Kendrea looked at me like, "Girl that's not due until next week." I told her I was struggling to even start and I could not wait until the weekend. I guess she saw the desperation in my eyes, because she took a deep breath and said, "Only for you Frenda. I guess this nap can wait." Kendrea shared with me the story of her name. The meaning of her name and its relation to her family's history. Needless to say, Kendrea's upbringing was very different from mine. For most of her life, she was raised with both parents. Her family lived in a few different places and they went on family vacations. We were excited about driving to Indiana Beach when I was younger. I guess that was the equivalent of a family vacation for us. Kendrea's story sounded like it could have been placed in a documentary and premiered on the OWN Network (well OWN didn't exist 20 years ago but you know what I mean).

Kendrea encouraged me to call my mom to discuss the assignment with her. She said, "Maybe you do not know all of the details behind your name. Why don't you call the one who named you? I am sure there is a story. There has to be with a name like yours." I called home, and I asked my mom, "Where did you get my name from?" She told me about a young lady who attended high school with her named, Frienda, spelled with an "i." She liked the name so she just kind of went with that name when she gave birth to me. I asked my mom if my name had anything to do with the fact that my dad's first name is Fernando. My mom swore she did not name me after my father. I still don't believe her. I think my name starts with an F because my dad's name starts with an F, I honestly do.

I am not exactly sure how our conversation got to my mom expressing how she had just finished high school when she found out she was pregnant with me. She went straight to working in order to save money in order to take care of me. At that time she could not depend on my father. My mom worked all the way up until she delivered me. I cannot imagine being pregnant at 18 or 19 years old and going through my first pregnancy without my mother (remember my mom's mother passed when she was 12). She had sisters, but they were all raising their own kids or living their own lives. My mom never mentioned any close friends when she was carrying me and let's just say we do not know where my father was at the time. I thanked my mom, first for all the sacrifices she made to take care of me. I then, thanked her for sharing her experiences during the time she carried me.

When you hear the name Frenda, what is the first thing you think about? A friend. I wrote my paper from the perspective of a 19 year old pregnant girl on the journey of both motherhood and womanhood, who lost her mother at the time she probably needed her the most and who had a sketchy relationship with the father of her unborn child. I think this was a very lonely time in my mother's life and she needed more than anything, a FRIEND.

I received an "A" on that assignment. I remember writing that paper over several times. I asked Kendrea to proof read it for grammatical errors. I also used some of the grammar pointers given to me by my English Professor. My professor returned my graded paper to me with a smile. My professor had something to smile about. As I stated earlier, she knew I struggled with grammar. She asked me to make an appointment to see her during her office hours on several occasions. I would always come up with an excuse as to why I had not come to see her during her office hours. Until one day she asked me to stay after class. I was both embarrassed and nervous. She asked me to sit down. "Listen, honey, I am here to help you. There is no need to be embarrassed." She was a Spelman alumnus so teaching at her alma mater meant the world to her. "I would like to invite you to my house on Sunday. We will attend church services, have Sunday dinner then we are going to work on your grammar." Before I could respond she said, "Be ready at 8:00 am, you live in LLC 1 correct?" I nodded my head. "I'll see you at 8:00 am on Sunday. I have to head out." As I am walking out of the classroom she says, "Honey, don't make me come in that dorm to get you. Just like I expect you to be on time for my class, I expect you to be right out front at 8:00 am Sunday." I responded, "Yes ma'am."

On Sundays (for that entire semester), I would go to church with my professor's family, we would have Sunday dinner, and after cleaning up we would work on grammar and writing techniques. I am forever grateful for my English professor, who after graduation became my Spelman sister. I credit her for my educational successes as well as for the assignment that began my journey of learning to embrace myself.

LIFE/MENTAL HEALTH TIP(S):
Never be embarrassed about who you are or where you come from. Be You. No one can be You better than You. Be unapologetically YOU!

Psalm 139:14 (NIV)
I praise you because I am fearfully and wonderfully made; your works are wonderful; I know that full well.

CHAPTER 3: MY MOMMY

I know I've talked a little bit about my mom when I discussed my name, but I decided to dedicate a chapter of my book to her. My mom is probably one of the strongest women I know. She's been through a lot. She lost her mother when she was 12 years old and was raised by her great-grandparents. My mom has 6 other siblings (my uncle passed a couple years ago) and she's the 6th child out of 7 children. My mom was very strict. As I got older, I realized she was strict as a way to protect us. My mom did not believe in allowing us to go over to others houses for sleepovers (unless it was with family). She allowed our friends to come over for sleepovers but we could not go to their houses.

My mom was very attentive, well as much as she could be even when she could not physically be in our presence. She asked us each day about school? My mom randomly called our teachers to simply check on us. I think my mom got saved (gave her life to Christ) when she was about 26 years old. I was about seven and my sister, Marquitta was five or six. We would wake up in the morning to her praying over us. I remember waking up to olive oil (referred to as blessed oil) running down our foreheads and my mom declaring prayers of protection over us.

Growing up, we went to elementary school in Maywood, which was a better school district than Chicago, from grades kindergarten to 3rd grade. We later attended grades 4th – 6th in Bellwood for that same reason. My mom would wake up, cook breakfast, wake us up and dress for work as we at breakfast. After we got dressed she would take us to either my maternal great-grandmother (Mama's) house (Maywood) or my paternal aunt's house (Bellwood) and we went to school from there. My mom would then, drive back to the city to go to work. In the evenings she left her job in the city, drove all the way back to the suburbs to pick us from Mama or my aunt's house, took us home back in the city, checked our homework, cooked dinner and got us ready to bed. She was my superhero.

As I stated before, my mom was very attentive. She did not let us out of her sight when we were with her. When she picked us up from Mama or my aunt's house, she asked us a ton of questions. I remember sitting on the floor in my mom's room as she was combing my hair. Out of the blue she says, "I know you be at that school cutting up. I know that you're on that playground fighting and cursing people out, so let this be a warning to you that I know all, and I see all. You can't hide nothing from me. I'm warning you! I am not going to whoop you this time, but if I find out that you've been fighting again on that playground and cursing people out, I'm gonna beat yo tail."

I sat there spooked, because in my mind I'm like, "Did my sister tell? Did my teacher call? Who told on me?" I was paranoid for a week. I was on the playground, making sure my sister wasn't watching me. She wasn't thinking about me. She was in her own world with her friends. A week later, on a Saturday morning, we were all sitting around laughing, eating and watching TV. Since my mom was in a good mood, I thought this would be the best time to ask, "Mom, remember when you said I was out on the playground fighting people and cursing? Who told you that? Did my teacher tell you?" I was like, "Did Quita tell you?" My mom looked at me and said, "Nope." I asked, "Well, who told you?" She looked me in my eyes and smirked, "The Holy Spirit."

That day I discovered a new fear, I was afraid of this Holy Spirit. The thought of this spirit following me around and tricking on me, had me scared. I knew God existed because my mom prayed all the time, but the Holy Spirit. Who the heck was that and why was he following me, ole snitch? I didn't ask her any more questions, I was too afraid. That day I made up in my mind, I did not want to have anything to with this spirit, holy or not.

As a little girl, I could sense when things were about to happen. It's like ever since my mom told me about that spirit; Holy or whatever his name was; I could feel when something was about to happen. I remember playing outside with my cousins when, all of sudden I heard, "Get in the house. Get all of your cousins and get in the house." I felt a sense of urgency. I remember yelling to my cousins, "Y'all, let's go play in the basement." When my cousins ignored me, I lied and told them Mama (my great-grandmother) said it was time to come in the house. They all walked slowly in the house, mad and on the verge of tears. As Mama is walking in the living room, I am trying to think of another lie to explain why we were all coming in the house. Before I could start my lie, we hear what sounds like a huge fight outside. Mama yells to all of the kids, "Go to the basement!" We run down to the basement screaming, we did not know why we were screaming. Well, we were screaming because Mama was screaming.

Later that day, I overheard my mom and aunts talking to Mama. There was a huge fight right in front of Mama's house involving my uncle Tee and one of my aunt's boyfriends. The boyfriend came to Mama's house in retaliation for my uncle who beat him for something he did or said to my aunt. My aunt's boyfriend came back for revenge with his friends and brothers. To make a long story short, what I felt was real. Whatever or whoever gave me the warning had to be real because we really were in danger. As intrigued as I was about what had happened, I did not share what I heard with my mom.

It wasn't until I started having "dreams while I was awake" did I think it was best to tell my mom what was happening to me. I was about nine years old. I was at my paternal aunt's house in Maywood. I was playing with my sister and cousins when I realized I had to go to the restroom. I rushed in the house, ran to the bathroom and plopped onto the toilet without closing the door. Once I realized I forgot to close the door, I went to stand up and everything around me froze. I could no longer hear the kids playing outside. I felt like everything around me was at a "stand-still" including me. Then all of sudden I heard a knock at the door. I tried with all my might to stand up again in an effort to the close the door but I could not move. My uncle, my aunt's husband, appears out of nowhere. He walks toward the front door. There's a loud blast, and my uncle is lying in the middle of the living room with glass all around him in a pool of blood.

I finally snap back to reality. I am sitting on the toilet with the door open but no one is in the house. I hop up and wash my hands. I walk slowly into the living room, there is nothing and no one there. I stand in my aunt's living room trying to make sense of what I thought I saw. After a few minutes I go back outside to play. A week or so later, my mom gets a call from my aunt. She's hysterical. My aunt is in the emergency room because my uncle was in a car accident. His body was ejected from the car. I could hear my mom saying, "So he was thrown from the car. He was lying there in blood with glass all over him." I ran to my room and put my bed covers over my head. I remember asking myself, "What the heck is happening to me??"

When my mom got off the phone with my aunt, I told her about my "dream while awake. "Mom, I've been having these, I don't know what to call them. But it like I'm dreaming but I am still awake." I explained to her what I saw with my uncle at my aunt's house. My mom explained that I was having visions. She spent the next hour talking to me about visions. My mom told me God allows people to see certain things to warn others. I wondered, "Why is God talking to me? I'm only nine. Nobody is going to listen to me. I'm a kid, so why would God show me? Who am I supposed to warn?"

After that day, I continued to have open visions. Whenever I had a vision, I would tell my Mom. I remember being outside playing at my house. There was a house across the street. It was a house filled with people; adults, children, men and women. Everybody lived in that house. The kids from that house would come across the street to play with us. We started to play a game of "It." As I was running to find a hiding spot, I freeze. In my mind, I'm saying, "Oh no, not again." All of the kids around me are froze. My attention is focused on the house across the street. It was like I was standing on the outside of the house but I could see inside of the house. People are fighting inside the house. In the middle of the living room, there's a mattress on the floor. There's a newborn baby on the mattress. In the middle of the fight, a lady is pushed down and she lands on the baby and the mattress. Everyone in the house starts screaming and crying. I snap back. The best way to describe the visions I would have as a kid is to think about the TV show, "That's So Raven." I would literally have visions like Raven Baxter.

Once I snapped back, I am in full-blown tears. I run into the house to my mom. She's like, "What happened? You out there fighting?" I'm like, "Mommy, that baby across the street is going to die." I just keep repeating, "The baby is going to die!" My mom was trying to calm me down. "I just had a dream while I was awake. They have to stop fighting so the baby will not die!" I finally calmed down after my mom promised she would talk to one of the ladies she knew who lived in that house. She promised she would warn her for me.

A week later, we pull up to our housing complex and there's an ambulance across the street. They are bringing out a stretcher. I start freaking out. My mom was like, "You guys stay in the car." She gets out. She's asking, "What happened? What happened?" One of the kids from the neighborhood says, "The baby got smashed." All I remember is screaming. After that day, I cried because I did not want to see or be warned about anything else. My mom tried to explain to me that this was a gift. It did not feel like I had a gift. It felt more like a curse. When I would feel myself going into one of those "dreams while awake;" I would close my eyes tight. However, it did not work, I could still see the scenes in my mind as clear as day. My mom tried to support me through my visions as much as she could. Every time I saw a vision, I ran to her crying and she would pray the peace of God over me. No one could pray peace over me like my mommy.

LIFE/MENTAL HEALTH TIP(S):
Give your parents a break. No, they are not perfect. They did not do everything correctly, but they gave all they knew how to give. Don't focus on the things you did not get from your parents. Do not concentrate on deficits. Rest and be assured that your parents could not give you what they did not have. Honor, love, and appreciate your parent(s) for attempting to provide you with all they could!

Exodus 20:12
Honor your father and your mother so that you may live long in the land the LORD your God is giving you.

CHAPTER 4: MY DADDY

I do not have many stories to share about my dad. It's not because I don't love him. I love him so very much. I just didn't grow up around him. Anything that I've learned over the years about my dad, I've learned as an adult. Although I grew up without the presence of my dad in my life, my mom made sure we spent time with my paternal side of the family. My sister and I spent a lot of time with my dad's mother, my granny. I love my granny so much. She's my only living grandparent. We also spent time with my paternal aunts, uncles, and cousins. My mom made sure she allowed us to visit our paternal side of the family when we were younger. We attended elementary school in Bellwood. We used my dad's sister, my aunt's address in order to be eligible to attend school in that school district. We also spent weekends and a few weeks out of the summer at my granny's house on the northwest side of Chicago.

We would sometimes see my dad at my granny's house. My mom and dad had no relationship when I was going up. There was no communication between them. I think they broke up when I was about three or four. My dad would always tell us to tell our mom, hi. As soon as my sister or I said, "Mommy, Mickey (that's my dad's nickname) said....." My mom would say, "Don't nobody want to hear anything Mickey has to say." My mom never said anything negative about my dad in our presence. However, we knew he was not her favorite person.

My mom did get upset at my dad and granny one time. We

were visiting my granny and my dad came over. He wanted to take us to the store with him. I was about seven, but I knew we were not supposed to go with anyone; including my dad. Remember, my mom was super-protective. We were given a pep talk every time we went to my granny, aunt or Mama (great-grandmother's) house. We were to stay with only those three ladies. We were not allow to go with anyone else. My dad told my granny that he was going to the store and he was taking his kids with him. He said he did not care what anyone had to say about it. I stood in my granny's living room conflicted and confused. My heart smiled at the thought of spending time with my dad but I was also thinking about the pep talks my mom gave us. My granny told me it was okay to go this time, but we would just keep it a secret between us. I was both reluctant and excited to go with my dad.

I was reluctant because I knew we were not supposed to go anywhere with anyone. However, I was happy to be with my dad. I was afraid of my mom finding out we went with my dad. I was also excited about spending time with my dad. When we got in the car, there was a girl around my age in the backseat. She smiled and beckoned for me to sit next to her. She introduced herself as Topeka. My dad told us, she was our sister. I was so nervous, but Topeka calmed my nerves. She was just smiling and talking to us. She was also playing a game of peek-a-boo with my sister. We were having so much fun, I didn't notice we had been to the store and was now back at granny's house. We stayed in the car with my dad's girlfriend, Ms. Debra (Topeka's mother) while my dad went inside the store and brought us all chips and candy. He gave us hugs and kisses and told us he loved us. My dad took us back to my granny's apartment. I remember being sad when he left.

My mom came to pick us the next day. A few days later; she randomly asked me, "Did you and your sister go to the store with Mickey?" I broke down and confessed. My granny must have felt bad about asking us to keep a secret from my mom, because she called my mom and told her. My mom was pissed. I remember her telling me, "Yeah, your grandma broke down and told me. I'm going to tell you, like I told her, you and your sister are not allowed to go anywhere with Mickey! Do not let me find out you went anywhere else with him, do you understand?" I nodded my head.

In my mind, I was like, "Why not?" But I was too afraid to actually ask my mom anything at that moment. I cannot remember if my dad ever tried to take us anywhere else after that, but I do remember never seeing my sister Topeka. We did reconnect as adults but I never saw her again during my childhood. I later learned that I had several other brothers and sisters on my dad side but I never met any of my siblings until adulthood. I never was afforded the opportunity to meet my brother Michael, he passed a few years ago. His funeral is where we connected with our siblings. We vowed that day to never disconnect from each other again.

When I got to college, I started to think about my dad a lot. I am not sure where these thoughts came from because at this point I had no relationship whatsoever with my dad. I think thoughts of my dad can possibly be contributed to the fact that I was really praying to God to help me with forgiveness. During my college years, I found myself desiring to really learn more about God. I grew up in church and I even prayed from time to time to God but I honestly did not know God. It was during those time when I sought God for clarity and began studying the Bible that I found myself thinking about my dad.

I was studying the subject of forgiveness a lot. I was trying to understand how forgiveness really worked or if it worked at all. I knew I had a lot of unforgiveness in my heart towards a lot of people. My unforgiveness record went all the back to age five when one of my aunt said some mean words about my mom in anger. Although I loved my aunt, I realized I had held a grudge against her for something she said like 15 years before. I was a grudge-holder. I was bitter. I had hate in my heart for others. I was full of revenge. The more I found myself desiring a closer relationship with God, the more I started to feel the weight of unforgiveness. Unforgiveness is heavy. It feels like a burden that zaps your energy and joy. No matter how great things were going in my life, happiness was always short-lived. I would wake up in the mornings sad but could never understand exactly what made me sad. I would go to bed at night tormented with thoughts of sadness and hopelessness. Unforgiveness had me in a very dark place.

My life at the time was blessed in so many ways but it was like I could not enjoy any of it. As I began to study the subject of forgiveness and the power that forgiveness holds, I remember asking God to help me to forgive my dad. I honestly did not think my dad was a bad person. I was just hurt because I often wondered why he was not in my life. One day I remember asking God to show me how to love my dad. I wanted to not only forgive him, I wanted to love him too. I did not just want to be able to say I loved my dad, I wanted to actually feel love in my heart for him. I wanted to love him like I loved my mom.

I started having dreams about moments I had with dad when I was younger. There was one dream where my mom, my dad, my sister and I were all in a big bed watching TV. I was maybe about three or four. My sister was younger because she had on a diaper. We were watching TV. My dad blew up a red balloon and I remember playing the game of trying to keep the balloon in the air. We laughed and hit the balloon back and forth for what seemed like hours. I remember waking up with a smile on my face. I honestly did not know if I made that dream up in my mind or if that moment had actually occurred. During a phone conversation with my mother later that week, I asked about where we lived when I was around age three or four. She told me we lived in a studio apartment on the Northside of Chicago. I asked her if my dad lived with us. She got really quiet for a minute. "Huh, why would you ask me that? That's so random. Where are all these questions coming from?" I told her about my dream. I was able to describe a few details of the apartment. When I described the big bed that sat in the middle of the room, I heard my mom whisper, "Oh my God, how do you remember that?' My mom told me my dad did not live with us but he did come over to visit when we were very young. He was actually very consistent with his visits until they officially broke up when I was about four years old. I had several more "dad moments" dream. I believe God heard my prayers as it related to my desire to forgive and love my dad. I believe God was bringing these positive memories of my dad back to my remembrance because God wanted me to see my dad's heart towards me. God wanted me to know that although he may not have been physically in my in life, for whatever reason, my dad loved me. He loved us (my sister, Marquitta and I).

During this time, I had several dreams about my dad. There is one in particular that prompted me to reach out to dad. I was at my granny's house. I was about five years old. I used to fake like I was asleep all the time. When I went to bed it was hard for me to go straight to sleep. It was like my brain would never calm down (my brain still works like this today). I would lie in bed daydreaming or thinking about a movie I had watched and when an adult would enter the room, I'd shut my eyes tight and act like I was asleep. I would fake snore and everything. In the dream, I was in my granny's room laying in her bed with my sister. Marquitta was probably about three years old. She was knocked out. My granny, one of my uncles, and two of my aunts were in the kitchen playing cards. My granny's bedroom was in the back near the kitchen. My granny had a dog named, "Lady." My sister and I were so afraid of "Lady." My granny would have to put her on the back porch when we visited because we would cry, run and hide when we saw her.

Everyone was in the kitchen; laughing, play cards and listening to music including "Lady." I heard her barking and people telling here to move. I hear someone enter the kitchen. Everybody was like, "Heyyyyyy." Then I heard my dad's voice. I sat up in the bed with a huge smile on my face, then I remembered I was supposed to me be "fake" sleep so I quickly laid back down. I remember hearing my granny say, "Your kids are here." My dad responded, "They are? Where?" My granny told him we were in her bedroom asleep. Then I heard my granny say, "Mickey, leave them alone. They're sleep." My dad said, "No, I need to see my babies." My dad entered the room and picked me up. He hugged me tight, I wanted to hug him back but I had to remember to "fake" sleep. He bends down and kissed my sister on her cheek. He takes me out into the kitchen area with everybody else. For a split second, I thought about "Lady" and I got scared. My dad starts rubbing my back and in an instant, my fears are gone. My dad sat at the table playing cards as I laid on him. My granny told him several times to go lay me down. He refused. I don't remember falling asleep, but I woke up the next morning looking for dad. I remember asking my granny "Granny, where's my dad?" She was like, "How do you know your dad was here? He was here last night, but he left. How do you know? He must've woke you up when he picked you up." I just kind of looked at her and I was like, "When is he coming back?" She responded, "Well, baby, I don't know. Do you want to eat?"

This particular dream prompted me to reach out to my dad. Initially, I was going to call him over the phone but then I thought about how much I wanted to share with him and I was not sure if I could get through it all over the phone; I decided to write him a letter. I sat down and wrote my dad a heartfelt letter. I expressed my desire to have him in my life. I told him I forgive him for whatever it was that kept him from being there for me. I wanted him to know that I was no longer holding on to the past and I wanted us to connect to get to know each as father and daughter. I got his address from one of my aunts and I mailed off the letter. I remember feeling like a weight lifted off my back once I put that letter in the mailbox.

A few weeks later, my dad called my phone. I missed the call because I was in class but he left a message. His message began with, 'Hey baby. It's your dad. I read your letter." There was a slight pause, "I love you and I am so sorry........ummm can you call me back when you get this message?" He left his phone number and before hanging up he told me he loved me again. I remember breaking down and crying. I cried for hours. But my tears were not tears of pain or hurt. My tears were tears of forgiveness and love. I called my dad after I thought I was finished with all of the tears. We talked, we laughed and we cried for hours.

I have been working to actively build a relationship with my dad since that day. I believe he has been working to do the same over the last 2 decades. I talk to and see my dad for time to time. We have celebrated a few Father's Days together. We have gone out to dinner and my dad has cooked for me and my siblings several times, he is an amazing chef. Over the past few years, I have gotten to know my dad on a more personal level. I have learned about some of his struggles that may have affected his ability to "father" and raise me when I was younger. I do not understand everything and I do not have answers to all of the questions that flood my mind at times. However, none of that matters. He is my dad. I love him. I honor him. I forgave him.

LIFE/MENTAL HEALTH TIP(S):

You do not always know the full story. Do not set your heart and mind to respond to a one-sided story. Learn to forgive even if you never receive the apology you think you deserve.

Matthew 6:14-15 (NIV)
For if you forgive other people when they sin against you, your heavenly Father will also forgive you. But if you do not forgive others their sins, your Father will not forgive your sins.

FORGIVENESS

What are the benefits of forgiving someone?

Letting go of grudges and bitterness can make way for improved health and peace of mind. Forgiveness can lead to:

- Healthier relationships
- Improved mental health
- Less anxiety, stress, and hostility
- Lower blood pressure
- Fewer symptoms of depression
- A stronger immune system
- Improved heart health
- Improved self-esteem

What are the effects of holding a grudge?
If you're unforgiving, you might:
- Bring anger and bitterness into every relationship and new experience
- Become so wrapped up in the wrong that you can't enjoy the present
- Become depressed or anxious
- Feel that your life lacks meaning or purpose, or that you're at odds with your spiritual beliefs
- Lose valuable and enriching connectedness with others

How do I reach a state of forgiveness?

Forgiveness is a commitment to a personalized process of change. To move from suffering to forgiveness, you might:

- Recognize the value of forgiveness and how it can improve your life
- Identify what needs healing and who needs to be forgiven and for what
- Consider joining a support group or seeing a counselor
- Acknowledge your emotions about the harm done to you and how they affect your behavior, and work to release them
- Choose to forgive the person who's offended you
- Move away from your role as victim and release the control and power the offending person and situation have had in your life

As you let go of grudges, you'll no longer define your life by how you've been hurt. You might even find compassion and understanding.

What happens if I can't forgive someone?

Forgiveness can be challenging, especially if the person who's hurt you doesn't admit wrong. If you find yourself stuck:

- Practice empathy. Try seeing the situation from the other person's point of view.
- Ask yourself why he or she would behave in such a way. Perhaps you would have reacted similarly if you faced the same situation.
- Reflect on times you've hurt others and on those who've forgiven you.
- Write in a journal, pray or use guided meditation — or talk with a person you've found to be wise and compassionate, such as a spiritual leader, a mental health provider, or an impartial loved one

or friend.

- Be aware that forgiveness is a process, and even small hurts may need to be revisited and forgiven over and over again.

Reference:

https://www.mayoclinic.org/healthy-lifestyle/adult-health/in-depth/forgiveness/art-20047692

CHAPTER 5: MY SELF-ESTEEM

I am reminded of the time I was about seven and my sister was about five or six. It was a Saturday morning and we were out shopping with my mom. My mom loved to shop. She could literally shop for hours. Because she worked so hard during the week, Saturday was her day to either relax or do what she loved, shop. So we are in a department store. My mom was in the dressing room trying on clothes and my sister and I were sitting on a small bench right outside of the dressing room area. Every 60 seconds my mom would yell out to us, "Frenda and Quita, y'all okay?" We would respond in unison, "Yes mommy."

One of the ladies working in the department store smiled at us and walked over to us. "You guys are sitting her so patient and quiet." We smiled but did not respond. We did not talk to strangers. My mom yells out again, "Frenda and Quita?" My sister responded, "Yes mommy?" My mom asked if we were okay. Again, we responded in unison, "Yes Mommy." The nice lady then looks at Marquitta and says, "You can go to the back with your mommy if you would like." My sister hops up and I get up behind her. As we are about to head to the back, the nice lady stops me. "I'm sorry sweetie, you can't go back there." Looking confused, I asked, "Why not?" The nice lady says, "Because you are a boy." Before I could respond, my sister turns back and says, "No she's not, that's my sister." The nice turned beet red. "Oh my gosh! Honey, I'm sorry. You have that hat on but now that I'm looking at you, I can see you are a pretty little girl." I ripped my skull cap off my head, revealing my bangs and three ponytails. The nice lady seemed to get more embarrassed. "I'm so sorry honey, you can go in the back with your mommy."

I remember it was cold that day so my sister and I had on coats, hats, gloves and scarves. I put my hat on that morning, making sure I covered my ears. My sister put her hat on but she took the time to pull her bangs out of the front of her hat. My mom would get upset with me for sloppily throwing on my winter attire. She would always try to fix my coat and readjust my hat because I just threw everything on. When we got into the dressing room with my mom, she noticed the look on my face. The nice lady calling me a boy had hurt my feelings. Although I was only seven, I remember not necessarily liking how I looked. I was tall and skinny with big teeth. My sister, Marquitta was short and cute. She had the cutest round face and cheeks. We were only 18 months apart but she was half my size. When we would visit family members, everyone was always so happy to see us. We would get a lot of hugs and attention but because Marquitta was so small and cute, everyone picked her and gave her extra hugs and kisses.

My mom asked me, "What's wrong with you? Why are you looking like that?" Before I could answer, my sister said, "That lady out there called her a boy!" My mom looked at me and shook her head. "You look nothing like a boy. What is she talking about?" I said, "Maybe because I had my hat on and I forgot pull my front bangs out." My mom looked at me and said, "See, this is why I tell you all the time. You didn't put any earrings in your ear when I told y'all to get ready this morning. Then you just threw on any ole outfit. I tell you all the time to be careful when you put your hat on so we will not mess up your hair and to brush your bangs down outside of your hat. You are always rushing. Now you see what I'm always talking about." I am sure my mom did not mean anything by the fussing out she gave me but at the moment, I did not need to be reminded of all those things. I sat down in the corner of the dressing room as my mom continued to try on clothes. My mom looked over in my direction, "You do not look like a boy, even with your hat on. I don't know what they lady was looking at….are you ready to go?" I nodded my head up and down. My mom started adjusting my coat and winter attire. She placed my hat over my head and combed through my bangs until my bangs were outside of my hat. "Let's go get some pizza." I smiled because I loved food but effects of that incident has stuck with me for years.

As I stated before, I never really thought of myself as pretty when I was younger. My mom dressed my sister and me alike all of the time in the cutest outfits. I would hear people tell my mom how pretty we were but I cannot remember a time as a young girl that I ever thought I was pretty. Issues of self-esteem worsen the older I got, especially once I hit puberty. I always felt awkward as a preteen. I was taller than my classmates. I was skinny and my feet were huge. I was also rather clumsy. It did not help that kids can be so cruel. I spent my days at school either beating someone up or threating them. I was going get them before they got me. I watched how classmates made fun of, laughed at and called others names. I decided I would beat you up before you could make fun of me.

I was a very smart student in school. However, my teachers hated to see me coming. I was B-A-D! My mom would punish me and spank me. I would be good for a day but the next day, I was right back at it. I was acting out because I did not like myself. I don't even know how a kid learns not to like themselves, but I was that kid. I got into fights all through elementary school. I even got suspended a few times. My mom got tired of spanking me and one day she broke down in tears and asked me what was wrong? She asked me if there was anything she did or did not do to make me act out at school. She pleaded with me to tell her what was going on. I remember crying because I hated to see my mom cry but I could not give her answer. I honestly did not know why I acted out at school. I felt like because I was always in trouble; that is what everyone expected of me. So I gave them what they expected and some times more.

My behavior did not change until my sister and I transferred schools. I was going to 7th grade and my sister was entering 6th grade. We would be attending a new school where no one knew who I was or what I had done in the past. I decided to turn over a new leaf. No more fighting. No more acting out. By this time, my sister had taken the "fighting' baton out of my hand. She was now the fighter in the family. Marquitta would fight any and everybody. She was short in height but that never fazed her. We later found out that my dad fought a lot growing up. My mom got into fights also but usually her fights were about defending one of her siblings or defending herself. My aunt told us, my dad had anger issues growing up. He would get angry and fight everybody. I think I was dealing with some anger issues of my own.

My behavior improved drastically once I entered 7th grade. I became a stellar student. I was praised for both my academics and behavior. Although my behavior had improved, I was still struggling with self-esteem issues. I still did not like how I looked. I hated my hair! It was nappy and unruly. My mom started perming my hair when I was about seven. My hair was so nappy, my mom still had to press my hair out when a "pressing" comb after perming it. I hated getting my hair done because the perm always burned my scalp. I would scream and cry. My mom hated doing my hair. She would try to warn me each time before she started the task. However, her warnings went out of the window once that perm or pressing comb got near my scalp. Out of frustration my mom spanked me but that only made things worse. I screamed even louder. The perm would leave painful scars in my head that hurt for weeks. If you think perming my hair was traumatic, "pressing" it was even worse. I was always getting burns from the "pressing" comb. I had burns on my ears, neck and my forehead because I could never sit still.

I started wearing braids when I got older to try to curb some of my hair issues. I was still getting perms to make my hair "manageable" for braids but I did not have to get perms as often with braids. I went all the way through college with my hair struggles. It was not until adulthood when I decided to stop fighting my hair and learn to embrace the hair I was blessed with. I decided to lock my hair with "sisterlocs." Several people tried to convince me not to do it but I was over the struggle and the opinions of others as it related to my hair. I have had my "sisterlocs" for 12 years and it was one of the best decisions of my life. My loc'tian, Sheena is amazing. She took me through a two week consultation to make sure I was ready to make the decision to lock my hair. When I decided to go forward in the process, she celebrated with me. She has been my loc'tian for the past 12 years. I love her. I love my hair.

LIFE/MENTAL HEALTH TIP(S):

Proverbs 31:25
She is clothed with strength and dignity, and she laughs without fear of the future.

SELF-ESTEEM
Self-esteem is how we value and perceive ourselves. It's based on our opinions and beliefs about ourselves, which can sometimes feel really difficult to change.

Your self-esteem can affect whether you:
- like and value yourself as a person

- are able to make decisions and assert yourself
- recognized your strengths and positives
- feel able to try new or difficult things
- show kindness towards yourself
- move past mistakes without blaming yourself unfairly
- take the time you need for yourself
- believe you matter and are good enough
- believe you deserve happiness.

What can cause low self-esteem?

The things that affect our self-esteem differ for everyone. Your self-esteem might change suddenly, or you might have had low self-esteem for a while – which might make it hard to recognize how you feel and make changes.

Difficult or stressful life experiences can often be a factor, such as:

- being bullied or abused
- experiencing prejudice, discrimination or stigma
- losing your job or difficulty finding employment
- problems at work or while studying
- ongoing stress
- physical health problems
- mental health problems
- relationship problems, separation or divorce
- worries about your appearance and body image
- problems with money or housing

How can I improve my self-esteem?

Be Kind to Yourself:

- Get to know yourself. Try to learn more about yourself – for example, what makes you happy and what you value in life. Some people say they find it helpful to write in a journal.

- Let yourself have feelings. It's important to remember that you're a human being who can experience a wide range of emotions.
- Consider what self-esteem means to you. You might realize you're basing your sense of self-worth on things that aren't useful or helpful for you.

Look After Yourself:

- Try to get enough sleep. Getting too little or too much sleep can have a big impact on how you feel.
- Think about your diet. Eating regularly and keeping your blood sugar stable can make a difference in your mood and energy levels.
- Try to do some physical activity. Exercise can be really helpful for your mental wellbeing, and some people find it helps improve their self-esteem.
- Spend time outside. Spending time in green space can help your wellbeing.
- Try to avoid recreational drugs and alcohol.

Try to notice the good things:

- Celebrate your successes. No matter how small they may seem, take time to praise yourself and notice what you did well. It could also help to remember past successes.
- Accept compliments. You could make a note of them to look over when you're feeling low or doubting yourself.
- Ask people what they like about you. It's likely that they see you differently to how you see yourself.

Build a support next work:

- Talk to someone. A friend. A mentor. A counselor. A therapist.
- Try peer support. Making connections with people who have similar or shared experiences can be

really helpful.

Learn to be assertive:

- Practice saying no. It could help to pause, take a breath and consider how you feel before agreeing to do something you don't want to.
- Give it time. Being assertive can feel difficult if you're not used to it, but it can feel liberating - and it gets easier the more you do it.
- Don't take too much on. It's ok to set boundaries around how much you do for other people. Over-stretching yourself to please others can drain your energy and affect your wellbeing.

Set Yourself A Challenge:

- Do things you enjoy. You could take up a hobby, learn something new, do a creative activity, or simply take the time to read a book or go for a walk.
- Try volunteering. You might decide to volunteer your time for something you feel passionate about.
- Set small goals, such as trying a recipe, learning the days of the week in a new language, or simply looking for information on something you'd like to do.

Reference:

https://www.mind.org.uk/information-support/tips-for-everyday-living/nature-and-mental-health/#.XhwSxSRMElQ

CHAPTER 6: MY MOLESTER

When I was about 11, maybe 12, my mom met my step-father. I can't remember the story behind how they met. But it wasn't a typical type of meeting. When you meet somebody through a friend or at a gas station or something like that, they met unconventionally. I can't remember exactly how, though. My mom started dating him, and he would come around. I was excited. Here was my chance to have a daily and present father, you know like all of the dads on TV. My step-father would bring gifts; he was so nice. We would all go out to eat together, participate in family activities, and sit around the table and eat dinner together. We never really did that before he came around. My mom cooked every day for us, but we would eat in front of the TV. Mom would eat quickly, then prepare for the next day. We would eat together sometimes when we went out, or perhaps on the weekend, but during the week, no. I remember watching families on TV sit down and eat dinner together. I remember wishing I could have a family like those. In my mind, I finally had one of those families.

My mom and step-father got married. I remember the day we found out. We were outside playing, and they called in, "Hey, we got to tell y'all something." And we were like, "Okay." They were like, "Oh, we got married." I was like, "Oh, okay, great." My sister was like, "When, how, where?" She had all the questions, but I was just sitting there like, "I can't believe I have a dad, a TV dad."

I started my menstruation when I was eleven. I did not have clue what was going with me. I remember being afraid of seeing all that blood but for some reason I did not tell my mom. I used tissue to try to control it. Of course, that was a disaster. My mom found out. She sat me down and explained what was going on with my body and showed me how to care for myself during that time each month. The first time I started my cycle, I felt a few small cramps. However the next month, I got really sick. I did not know what was going on. I had the worst cramps ever. I could not keep food or liquids down. I think I vomited for seven days straight. Each month after that I got the same results. I hated that time of the month. I would cry a week before my cycle in anticipation of the pain and torment.

The average cycle for most women lasts three to four days. For me, it was seven days of bleeding. It was seven days of throwing up. I couldn't keep any food down. I would literally be out of my mind. I was in so much pain. I attempted suicide a couple of times. That's how much pain I was in. I not only had to deal with physical pain, I had to endure mental torment. I would hear voices. The voices would tell me to hurt myself. So not only am I sick, throwing up for seven days straight. I dreaded this time of the month. I cried because the pain and the torment that I was dealing with was just unbearable. The voices would say to me, "Go in the kitchen, get a knife," "Throw yourself down the stairs," or "Jump out this window." Every month, my mom took me to the doctor because she felt like I was losing too much blood.

My mom would tell the doctors, "She's losing blood, she's delirious. Sometimes she's completely out of her mind. This is not normal!" Each month, the doctors would try to ensure that I was going to be okay; some young ladies experience the symptoms of their cycles worse than others. Doctors would prescribe liquid Motrin because I had a hard time swallowing pills. Something the liquid medicine would work for the pain, but most times I couldn't even keep that down. I would throw everything up. It was mental and physical torment. I would mark my calendar each month. I would try to prepare myself mentally. My mom would be like, "You have to fight," and "You have to pray and ask God to heal you." I remember my mom would have me sleep in the room with her so she could watch me during the night. It was during the night when I would hear voices and attempt to hurt myself. My mom had to hide all of the knives and sharp objects. After the seven days of "hell," I would go back to school, get all of my work made up, go right back to being a leader, go back to sports, and go back to everything like nothing happened. I just went right back to my regular life.

Amid my monthly torment, my mom married my step-father. So now he's in the house, and he's trying to assist and help during these tormenting times for me. My step-father would ask my mom, "What can I do to help?" He would do his best to comfort me and help in any way he could. I started having dreams that I was being touched inappropriately by my step-father. Well, I thought I was dreaming. I tried to block the thoughts from my mind. I convinced myself that I was dreaming. This is the man that came into my life, my mom's life, and my sister's life to love and take care of us. He would never hurt us. I tried to make sense of the dreams by blaming the books I was reading and the movies I was watching. I was a bit of a loner, so I read a lot and watched lots of movies. I would watch TV all day if I could. After I completed my homework, I watched TV; I watch all kind of movies or I read all types of books. I would have these recurring dreams of him touching me. I was trying to convince myself this did not happen. I would find myself saying, "You tripping, Frenda. You're making stuff up in your mind. Just like the voices that you hear are made up."

There was a time when I was at the end part of my seven days of "hell." I wasn't throwing up, but I was in pain from the days of throwing up. I could keep down liquid, so I may have been drinking Ginger Ale. I don't think I was eating food, but I'm like, "Okay, it's coming to an end. This pain is subsiding. I got probably another day of this pain, and then I'll go back to my regular life." I'm asleep in my room. It had to be the weekend, because my mom and my sister were out shopping. My step-father was downstairs watching TV. I am sleep but still was aware of my surroundings. I hear the door open. I do not know why, but I remember being scared and closing my eyes tight and pretending I was sleeping. In my mind, I keep telling myself, "He's just here to check on me and to make sure I'm okay. Once he sees that I'm okay, he's going to leave."

He didn't leave. He walks over to my bed and he whisper my name. He called my name a couple of times, but I didn't respond. I kept acting like I was sleep. By this time, I can feel him standing over me. He takes a seat at the edge of my bed. He starts to pull down my shorts and underwear and started touching me. "It wasn't a dream. He has been doing this to me." I quickly opened my eyes and sat up. He looks at me, and he's like, "What's wrong with you? What's wrong with you?" I stare at him with tears in my eyes. He is silent. He stands up, he leaves out of the room, and goes back downstairs to watch TV. I burst out in tears. I slowly get up and lock my door. I wait for my sister and mom to return. When my mom and sister returned, my sister comes upstairs to check on me. She tries to open the door, but I forgot I locked it. I get up slowly to unlock the door. As I open the door, she's like, "why did you lock the door?" I didn't respond. She notices my eyes are red, and she's like, "Oh my God, you're still sick. Oh my God, I figured you'd be okay. I bought you some fruit. I bought you this because I figured you would be able to eat something." I told her I wasn't hungry. That day, I didn't say anything to my sister or my mom.

A few months passed. My step-father did not try anything during those months. I figured he realized I was not out of it the last time he tried to touch me, so he would never do it again. I was intentional about making sure to sleep with my mother during my cycle, so my step-father would be forced to sleep downstairs. I remember a time when my mom wanted to go to the store, and I pleaded with my sister to stay with me. I was doing my best to stay away from my step-father during this time of the month. My plan was working until I started my cycle on the day I "supposedly" had an interview with a Catholic high school my step-father applied to on my behalf. I was a very smart student in middle school. I was at the top of my class. So when it was time for high school, I didn't want to go to the neighborhood school (Crane High School). I wanted attend a school like the ones my middle school teachers talked about; selective enrollment, magnet or private. My step-father always spoke about his connections with Catholic schools and about people he knew who could help me get into an excellent high school.

So on this day, I had an interview with a Catholic high school, but I got sick. My cycle came earlier than expected. I was in my room sleep. I remember my mom talking to my step-father, and she's like, "Well she can't go, look at her she's sick. Her cycle came on. She's been throwing up all night; she can hardly move. So she is going to have to miss this interview." I remember my step-father telling my mom, "She can't miss this one because if she misses this one, she's not going to get into the school." My mom is like, "How is she going to interview throwing up, how?" Somehow my step-father convinced my mom to let him take me to this interview. I remember my mom helping me get dressed. I put a peppermint in my mouth, and my mom's like, "I know you're not feeling good, baby. But you have this interview if you want to get into this school. You said you do not want to go to Crane so you have try to get to this interview." I kept telling my mom, "I want to lay down. I don't feel good." She hugged me and said, "I know, I know. It is only going to take an hour or so, and he'll bring you right back." I get in the car with my step-father, and he takes me to a hotel. Yes, you read that correctly, he took me to a hotel. I know for a fact that I was not out of my mind that day because about two months later, my mom was driving. We are from the west side of Chicago. We were driving down Pershing Road on the Southside, and I looked over and see that same hotel. Without really thinking, I blurted out, "Oh, there's that hotel right there."

My mom hit her breaks because she almost hit something. She looks back and says, "How do you know that's a hotel? How do you know that?" I just looked at her. I didn't say anything. Then I said, "Mom, it says hotel on the building." We did not talk for the remainder of the trip, but I would catch her staring at me through the mirror. So my step-father takes me to this hotel, he undresses me. I'm sick and trying not to vomit. I'm not feeling well, but I'm in my right mind. He says, "I brought you here so you can take a nice hot bath and get some rest." This was during a time when our heat and gas was disconnected. We were using electric heaters and boiling water to take baths.

Let me pause right here to say. My sister and I never knew what it was like to "go without," so to speak. We had everything we needed growing up. We had an abundance. If my mom did not have something, we never knew because we almost always got not only what we needed, but also what we. It was like once my mom married my step-father, we went from having an abundance to struggling. She stopped working, I think, when she got pregnant with my little sister. He filled the bathtub with water and I got in the tub. He was like saying, "I know this will make you feel better. This hot water will help your cramps. You are sick but can't even really take a hot bath." I remember looking at him, and I said, "Well, why didn't you just bring my mom and my sisters here, too, so we all could take baths? You said I was going on an interview, but I'm here." He was like, "Well, I just wanted to bring you here so you can feel better. So you can bath in hot water." I mumbled, "I'm sure my mom and sisters probably would have loved to take hot baths too." I get in the tub, I get out and dry off. I go to put my clothes on. He's like, "No, don't put your clothes on. I'm going to lay a towel on the bed. You just lay here under the covers and just rest." I obeyed. I laid on the bed with a towel and covered myself up. He says, "I'm about to go to the store. Do you want anything?" I'm like, "I can't eat anything. I've been throwing up." When he leaves out, I get up and quickly put my clothes back on. I get back in the bed, fully clothed. When he comes back, he's mad. He's like, "Why would you put your clothes on and lay in this bed with these outside clothes on?" I'm like, "I don't feel comfortable laying in this bed with no clothes on. I don't feel comfortable being here. Can you please take me home?"

By this time, he was pissed. At this point, I do not care. I wasn't feeling good, I was tired, and I wanted to go home. We get in the car, and as he is taking me back home he says something to the effect of, "I'm just trying to be a good dad to you. I want you to feel better because you were sick. You don't appreciate stuff that I do for you." He continues to talk, but I am so tired I am in and out of sleep. I remember waking up to him, saying, "If you say something to your mom, you going to mess up our family." I remember before I got out of the car looking at him. I said, "I'm not going to say anything. I just will never go anywhere else with you." That was the day when I decided to hate him. I hated him like I had never hated anyone ever in life. I was weak and sick but I remember thinking, "You have really been touching me. Here I was thinking I was dreaming or that something was wrong with me for thinking you could do something like this...... to someone you claim is your daughter. Then you manipulated my mom into letting you leave the house with me while I was sick just to take me a hotel." I honestly do not know what he was planning to do to be me at that hotel.

I do know, I messed up whatever plans he had when he returned to the hotel room from the store and I was fully clothed. I don't even know what type of story he made up about the "supposed" school interview. I came into the house; my mom was like, "You okay?" She asked me a few questions as she helped me take off my coat, but I did not respond. She told me to go lay down in her bed. Again, still today, I do not know what story he told her about that fake school interview. Whatever story he told my mom, she was not buying it. I remember her later questioning me about it, and I would just say, "I don't remember." She would be like, "I just don't believe that you don't remember." I feel like she could sense something was off, but she just couldn't put her finger on it.

After the hotel incident, I stayed away from my step-father. I would literally walk past him in the house and not acknowledge him. During that time of the month, I would ask to sleep in my mom's bed, or I would make sure my sister stay with me. My sister could not go anywhere. I would make her sleep in the same bed with me. She'd get up to go to the bathroom and I'd be like, "Where are you going? You have to stay with me." That was my way of trying to protect myself. There were a few times when I would overhear my step-father telling my mom, "I found this razor, Frenda was trying to cut herself." By this time, I didn't hear voices as much during my cycles. I remember during those times, praying to God to help me stay in my "right mind." I asked God to protect me from my step-father during my cycle. I remember even praying for the protection of my sister, Marquitta. I believe God answered my prayers. I would be sick, but it was like I wasn't out of my mind anymore.

I would still get sick. I'd be vomiting, but I could talk, I could tell you what was going on. Beforehand, I could not, I was just kind of loopy. My step-father would tell my mom, "Frenda had this razor. I just took it from her," and my mom would be like, "Where did she get it from?" She would go into panic mode like, "I thought I hid everything sharp." Remember, there was a time when I would try to harm myself. However, I had not dealt with suicide ideations in months. He was lying. I guess he was trying to build a case for himself, just in case I told my mom what he done to me.

The day that I decided to tell, I told my sister, not my mama. I was 14 by this time and I was in my freshman year of high school. My step-father did not have an opportunity to touch me again after the hotel incident. I continued to stay close to my mom and sister during my cycle. One day, my mom was like, "Each time you get sick, you have to sleep in my bed, and your step-father has to sleep downstairs. Go sleep in your bed and I will check on you throughout the night." I think I may have cried so my mom came in my room with me until I went to sleep. Every night after that I locked my door or slept in the bed with my sister. I remember being so anxious during this time of the month.

One this particular day, I was not feeling well. I was downstairs. I refused to go upstairs to sleep. I was sleeping in the living room. I was crying and my sister came and sat next to me. She looked at me and she whispered "I know." She looked at me, and she said, "I know something isn't right.....I know something's going on, and I just need you to tell me so that I can tell mommy." I was like, "What are you talking about?" She kept saying, "I know." She looked right at me, and she was like, "I know....I already know, I just need to hear you say it." I started crying. I was relieved. Finally, I could tell somebody. Although I felt some relief after telling the truth about what had happened to me, I also found myself feeling bad because "I was about to mess up our family. I was about to single-handedly destroy my family." I just looked down, and I said, "He has been touching me for a while now and taking my clothes off and doing all kinds of sexual stuff. It's been happening. At first, I thought it was like a dream because I'd be out of my mind or whatever. But there are times when I was not out of it and he touched me, so I know for a fact he has been touching me."

My sister started crying. We both cried. My mom came home. I think she was out grocery shopping. I don't even know where my step-father was at this time. They were having their own issues, so I don't know if he was at work or taking a few days to cool off (he would do that from time to time). By this time, my baby sister, Victoria, was already born. My mom might have been pregnant with my brother, Joshua. She ended up miscarrying right before his due date. I finally told my mom. She was hurt. She was pissed. She called him and went off on him over the phone. She put him out of the house. She kept apologizing to me. She would ask me questions about why I didn't tell? I just really couldn't, I didn't have answers for why I didn't fight back. I could tell she was wrecking her brain trying to figure out how she missed it. We would go days just crying. I would hear her crying in her room at night.

My step-father denied ever touching me. He called me a liar and said I was crazy. I remember my mother trying to get to the bottom of what happened. We even went to the Pastor of the church we were attending at the time, for what I guess was supposed to be family counseling. We sat there in the Pastor's office. My mom was crying. My step-father was there in a suit and tie trying to speak proper. He didn't even attend church, but he visited occasionally. I remember my mom telling the Pastor, "My daughter is saying my husband did this stuff, and he's saying that he did not." My mom was like, "I'm in the middle of this. My daughter doesn't have a reason to lie, but you know, I'm just.....I'm so confused." Nothing really came out of pastoral counseling or whatever it was. It was just more so of the Pastor giving advice to the family. I remember the Pastor looking me in my eyes and telling me to make sure I dressed appropriately when my step-father was around.

I maybe one-sided in my perception of the situation, but when I heard that from the Pastor's mouth, I immediately shut down. I remember thinking to myself, "This is why I didn't want to tell. Now my mom is questioning whether I'm telling the truth, my step-father is telling blatant lies," and now this pastor is saying, "Well, I don't know who to believe, but young lady you just make sure you dress appropriately in the presence of your step-father. Make sure you are covered up. He told my step-father to make sure he was never alone with me in the house." I was devastated. I was angry. I was hurt. Here I am already dealing with identity issues, insecurities, sickness, molested by the man that was supposed to love and protect me; and now a Pastor was talking to me like I was at fault for being violated. I went into a deep depression. I regularly attended school but as soon as I got home, I got in the bed and slept until the next day.

My sister from day one believed me. She was like it makes sense because my step-father always talked about how much my sister talked too much. He was always saying she couldn't keep her mouth closed. My step-father would do things like, if he gave us money, he would secretly give me more. I remember getting money from my step-father for doing chores and he would slip me an extra $20 and say I did a better job with my chores than my sister did. I never really spent the money, I would put it in a coat pocket and hide it in the back of the closet.

I remember my mama needed money for something. She was sitting at the table stressed about a bill or something and I pulled almost $200 out of that coat pocket. I saved almost all of it. My sister would get money, and she'd buy candy and snacks. When I handed my mom the money, she looked at me like, "Where did you get this from?" I said, "Every time I get money, I just put it in my coat that is in the back of the closet." My mom just stared at me. At the time I gave her the money, she didn't know anything about the molestation. I think her mind started going back to certain incidences once I told her what my step-father had done. Her mind went back to the time I pointed out that hotel. I know she was thinking, "You had all this money in that coat pocket, like where were you getting this money from? Her mind went back to the time when he "supposedly" took me to that interview when I was sick. My mom just kept remembering incident after incident. It was now all making sense.

My mom was hurt. At the same time, she was apologizing to me because she didn't know. I was like, "Mom, it's not your fault. You just didn't know." It was just a lot. My mom was trying to care for three kids, deal with the loss of a baby, and she was dealing with the knowledge of her husband molested her daughter. He still denied it. I found myself having feelings of shame and condemnation. I would come up with ways to blame myself daily. A mistrust for men formed in my heart, and I just remember making several vows to myself. I would never allow anyone to hurt me, touch me, and/or lie on me again. I needed to protect myself. I was trying to deal with everything on my own. I never went to counseling, other than whatever that was at the church. Nobody at school knew. Nobody in my family knew. It became a family secret. I could not talk to anyone so I kept everything bottled up inside. I dealt with a lot of shame and condemnation. Why didn't you tell in the beginning? Why didn't you fight him off? Did you want this to happen? Where you asking for it? There were all kinds of things going on in my mind. I felt like I was going to lose my mind. When a child is violated at age three, or five or even seven; they are too young to fight and defend themselves. I was old enough to do something and because I did not, I blamed myself. In my mind, it was my fault.

LIFE/MENTAL HEALTH TIP(S):
It was not my fault and if it happened to you, it was not your fault either! There was nothing you did to deserve abuse. There was nothing you could have done to stop the abuse. The first steps to healing are; (1) acknowledge that the abuse happened and (2) seek help through counseling and/or therapy.

Isaiah 43:2-3a
When you go through deep waters, I will be with you. When you go through rivers of difficulty, you will not drown. When you walk through the fire of oppression, you will not be burned up; the flames will not consume you. For I am the Lord, your God.

Childhood Sexual Abuse
Sexual abuse in childhood can leave scars that can last for a long time. Some people feel terrified about reporting abuse. They may feel embarrassed, guilty, or ashamed. Some people blame themselves or believe that they deserved to be abused. Others report abuse, but they aren't taken seriously or believed. Sexual abuse is a crime. It can have a large impact on health and well-being.

How does childhood sexual abuse affect adult well-being?

Childhood sexual abuse can have a wide range of effects in adulthood. Some adult survivors experience few mental health problems, while others experience many mental health problems. Abuse is a kind of trauma. Trauma is a situation that's shocking, intense, and distressing.

The effects of trauma include a complicated mix of factors, such as:

- The amount of any kind of trauma you previously experienced
- The severity of the trauma
- How close you were to the person who abused you
- How long the abuse lasted
- How people you trusted reacted to the abuse if you told them—did they believe you and support you or dismiss you?

Here are some of the ways that experiences of childhood sexual abuse can affect well-being:

- Trust—Abuse may impair your sense that the world is a safe place and impair your ability to trust others. This may be particularly difficult if you had a close relationship with the abuser.
- Self-esteem—you may blame yourself for the abuse, even though it isn't your fault. You may have a hard time feeling good about yourself or hopeful about your future.
- Coping with stress—you may have a lot of negative feelings, which may make it hard to cope with everyday stress.
- Impulsivity—Impulsivity means acting on urges before thinking through the consequences, which can lead to risky activities.
- Anger—you may have a hard time controlling your anger.
- Dissociation—with dissociation, your mind "separates" itself from painful events to protect itself. You may have a hard time remembering what happened, feel like the world around you isn't real, or feel like you aren't connected to your body. It's a common reaction to pain and fear.
- Self-harm—you may harm yourself, but not intend to end your life. It may be a way to cope with

difficult thoughts or feelings.

What can I do about it?

It's important to find help as soon as you can. Connecting with others who care about and support you as early as possible can help protect you from the negative impact of childhood sexual abuse and help you heal. Unfortunately, many people feel that talking about childhood sexual abuse is taboo, even though we know it happens and know that it's a crime. Some survivors are cut off from supports like family, friends, and community members when they talk about their experiences. This isolation can make it harder to heal and feel well again.

You can find help for problems associated with childhood sexual abuse. Treatment for adult survivors may help you:

- Overcome troubling thoughts and feelings, like self-blame, guilt or low self-esteem
- Overcome unhelpful coping strategies, like self-harm or eating problems
- Build healthy skills, like building trust and setting healthy boundaries in relationships
- Treatment should also address any other mental health or substance use problems, so it will look different for everyone.
- Remember, you may have experienced traumatic events in the past, but people can help now. It is never too late to find help.

Reference:

https://www.heretohelp.bc.ca/infosheet/childhood-sexual-abuse-a-mental-health-issue

CHAPTER 7: MY ADOLESCENCE

My adolescent years were a very dark time for me. However, amid all the stuff I was dealing with, I was favored. For some reason, I always found favor with teachers, mentors, and administrators. Although I was struggling with issues of identity and self-esteem, fighting through the shame of molestation and facing monthly cycles of sickness; I excelled at school. If there was a contest and I entered it, I almost always won. If there was a raffle and I was there, the number pulled was almost always mine. I was also randomly picked out in crowds like, "You, right there. Yes, you come here."

I remember when I was about 13 years old and I was at church. It was a prophetic revival or some kind of special service. There was a prophetess by the name of Nina Marie Leslie. I'll never forget her. I think God connected us that day. We later built a mentorship, friendship type of relationship. I looked up to her. That night, she randomly asked everyone that had on yellow to come up front. I had on a pair of big yellow shorts, and I could not hide. Prophetess Nina Marie prophesied to everybody in yellow. What was so crazy about this situation was, I had a summer job. It was my first job, so every Sunday, I looked forward to picking out my outfits for the week. I had specific outfits assigned to particular days. I remember waking up that morning, and I could not find my outfit for Wednesday.

After searching for 15 minutes, I was forced to wear my "Thursday" outfit on "Wednesday." I was pissed. I had a way of thinking and planning, and if things did not go as planned,

I would lose it. When Prophetess Nina Marie asked everybody in yellow to come up front, my first thought was, "I was supposed to wear yellow tomorrow." There was a line of approximately ten people, she prophesied to everybody. I was the last person in line. I was also the only kid in this line. She gets to me, and when I say this woman prophesied my life from high school through college. She tells me, "You're going to excel in high school and college." She was like, "You're going to have a high GPA. God wants to take you somewhere educationally." She said, "Whatever college you desire to attend, don't lose that desire. That's the college God wants to set you up at. People are going to tell you that you can't get into that college. It's going to be God that puts you there because it's a setup. God needs to set you up in certain environments for what he wants to do with your life."

She warned me about a young man who would come to try to get me off focus and altar my life in a negative way. "He's coming, and you're going to like him. Don't date him. Steer clear of this young man." She gave me the name of the guy and everything. Although I was familiar with the prophetic, I was spooked. She went on to discuss my college years and how I would graduate and put me in the college and how God was going to use me to be the first in my family accomplish several things. I just remember crying because she was prophesying my dreams and many desires I had in my heart that I never shared with anyone. She just kept prophesying to and then she said, "Even for college you won't have to pay for anything." Of course, my mommy is crying, and Prophetess Nina Marie was shouting, "God is going to take good care of you."

I go through high school. As stated before, I started high school late. I got accepted to several magnet schools, but they were not in my neighborhood. At the time, my mom could not afford to give me bus fare to travel to and from school every day. She just didn't have the money. She told me, "you going to have to go to a school close enough to walk, because we don't have the money for bus fare or I can't drive you every day to school." Of course, I was devastated because, and at my elementary school, Washington Irving, I was a stellar student. I was a leader. If the adults wanted to get a message down to my peers, they would tell me, and I would convince my peers to follow suit. Now that I think back on everything, I was used as a pawn in many incidents by adults when I was in middle school. I was young. I didn't know the same teachers who claimed they cared for me, was using me.

When it was time for eighth-grade graduation, I was supposed to be valedictorian. I earned it. However, that honor was given to another student. I felt cheated. It's a long story that I do not care to get into because I still legit get mad when I think about it. I ended up not even going to my eighth-grade graduation because I was sick. My cycle came on and could not stop vomiting. I missed my graduation. I was listed as the salutatorian, and I was supposed to deliver the welcome speech for graduation. The school thought that my mom kept me away from the ceremony because she was upset about me not being valedictorian, but that wasn't true. My mom spent money on a cute outfit from Lord & Taylor. I had my hair done, nails painted, and my mom was going to allow me to wear a little lip-gloss that day. But I literally could not walk or talk because I was vomiting. I spent that summer trying to work and figure my way out of going to Crane High School, the neighborhood school. I heard awful stories about Crane, specifically the gang fights that would randomly take place. I was so scared. So when I heard my mom utter the words, "Frenda, you're going to have to go to Crane," I was devastated. I could not sleep or eat.

I visited the library faithfully each week. I would check out 4-5 books each time, and once I read them all, I'd go back to pick out 4 or 5 more. I use to love to escape life through reading books. One day while walking to the library, I noticed a big school building on Adams right across from the park. I did some research and found out it was high school, and although enrollment was low, it was open and accepting applications for incoming freshmen. I pleaded with my mom to allow me to attend this school (that I did not know anything about) instead of Crane.

Out of pity, my mom allowed me to attend to Cregier High School. Cregier was a little rinky-dink school that probably should have closed years before I got there. The school was cold and dark. The teachers sat like statues, reading novels, or talking on their phones while we completed elementary school level worksheets. I didn't start until like October. Although I missed an entire month of school, I made up all missing assignments in a week. I promise I did. I asked the teachers for every assignment I missed; they were looking at me like I was crazy. "You wasn't here to learn what we taught," I looked at the assignments and I said, "I'll figure it out." I did just that. I would finish the class assignments in 15 minutes and spend the remainder of that class time reading library books. Every assignment or project, I excelled in it. I received straight A's. I started tutoring and helping my peers with tasks. I even graded papers for several teachers each week. The principal who was rarely in attendance called me into his office one day. He sat and stared at me for a few minutes. I was so uncomfortable. I felt the same nervousness I felt around my step-father. He looked me in my eyes and asked me, "Why are you here? Why are you at this school? We are all confused about why you here." I just looked at him and told him; I was afraid to go to Crane. He mumbled something like, "sorry, but you may end up there after all. We are closing at the end of the year, and all students will transfer to Crane." My heart dropped. I guessed he noticed the look on my face because he said, "no worries, I know the principal over there. I'll tell him all about the smartest student that I've met in years. He will take care of you."

Although I didn't necessarily trust that principal, his words calmed me. I was not super excited about attending Crane, but I was no longer afraid. Anything had to be better than Cregier. My younger sister, Marquitta, was graduating from eighth grade so she would be attending Crane also. My sister was cool with attending Crane. She was happy that the school was right up the street, we had a long walk to get to our middle school. The next school year, my sister and I entered Crane High School, ready for whatever. I think she was more excited than I was. As a sophomore, I entered with my 4.0 GPA and took the #1 sophomore rank. There were a few students pissed off about that, but I held my own academically, even at Crane. I joined the Academic Decathlon team. I met one of my life mentors, Dr. Williams. I met teachers who took the time to invest in me, and when they saw that I was a quick learner even in the honors program, they introduced me to extracurricular enrichment programs to help challenge me. I met some great teachers who, when they saw that I was different, they took the time to try to give me more challenging projects and assignments.

One of my teachers, Miss White, taught English. We spent time each day in English class competing worksheets on grammar. While the other students were working on grammar, she introduced me to Shakespeare. It was so hard because although I was an avid reader, I had never read anything like it. I read romance and urban novels. When I would get frustrated, she would say, "I know it's hard, but I need you to read this book because I know you're going to go to college, and you're going to have to get used to reading books you do not enjoy. You are going to have to read them, and you will have to learn to comprehend what you are reading." She would give me extra assignments and additional projects. I appreciate her for taking the time to attempt to prepare for college. Dr. Williams, she was our Academic Decathlon coach. Sh introduced me to several opportunities outside of Crane. There was an enrichment program I participated in for three summers at Wheaton College. Project SOAR was a STEM program for minorities. We lived on campus, we took classes and participated in enrichment activities. We also received a stipend for attending. Dr. Williams introduced me to a lot of events in Chicago, like the Black Women's Expo and Auto Show. I would work at these events each year and receive a stipend. She would expose us to so many activities and programs around Chicago.

I can honestly say, attending Crane High School was one of the best decisions of my life. Because I was able to shine and stand out in that environment, I was blessed with many opportunities to represent my school as a peer leader and as the Local School Council student representative. I also played basketball, and I was captain of the Academic Decathlon team.. I was not the best basketball player, but Coach Phil took us to places all over the state of Illinois to play ball. Although Crane was a neighborhood school, I will forever be grateful for the support, encouragement, and investment from staff members like Principal Melver Scott, Dr. Williams, Miss White, Counselor Deloney, and Coach Phil (just to name a few).. Everything wasn't perfect at Crane. Trust me, we had our share of issues and problems, but honestly speaking, Crane was absolutely the best place for me.

LIFE/MENTAL HEALTH TIP(S):

Job 10:12 (KJV)
You have granted me life and favor, and your care has preserved my spirit.

5 Truths about the Favor of God

What would your life be like if the favor of God surrounded you each and every day? Would you experience more grace? More happiness? More success? Would the fruit of the spirit (Galatians 5:22-23) be more evident in your life? If you want to experience more of the favor of God, then embrace these five truths:

Truth #1: God's Favor *is* God's grace.

"For by grace you have been saved through faith, and that not of yourselves; it is the gift of God." –Ephesians 2:8, *NKJV*

God's favor, aka God's grace, is the reason you are saved. You are saved by His favor.

Truth #2: God's favor affects every area of life.

"So God can point to us in all future ages as examples of the incredible wealth of his grace and kindness toward us, as shown in all he has done for us who are united with Christ Jesus." –Ephesians 2:7

God's favor has taken care of everything you will ever need—spirit, soul and body. Every part of your life is impacted by the grace and favor of God. This doesn't just mean you are going to heaven. It means you are delivered, protected, preserved, healed and made whole.

Truth #3: God began showing you His favor even before you were born again.

"But God showed his great love for us by sending Christ to die for us while we were still sinners." –Romans 5:8

Salvation is the greatest expression of God's favor, and it was made available to you even when you were still lost. Being born again was just the starting place for His favor to pour out. And He will pour out grace and more favor to you every moment of your life if you'll receive it!

Truth #4: God's favor surrounds you continually.

"For You, O Lord, will bless the righteous; with favor you will surround him as with a shield." –Psalm 5:12, *NKJV*

As a born-again child of God, you have been made righteous by Jesus and that righteousness came with the favor of God, which surrounds you constantly!

Truth #5: You must realize and accept God's favor to experience it fully.

"May God give you more and more grace and peace as you grow in your knowledge of God and Jesus our Lord. By his divine power, God has given us everything we need for living a godly life. We have received all of this by coming to know him, the one who called us to himself by means of his marvelous glory and excellence." –2 Peter 1:2-3

If you desire to have God's favor evident in your life, then begin to study and contemplate these truths. Understand that God's favor—His grace—was available to you even before you were His. And now, since you are a child of God, His favor toward you has grown. It touches every area of your life and surrounds you continually. All you have to do is accept it by faith. The favor of God is yours—now and forever.

Reference:

https://www.kcm.org/real-help/spiritual-growth/learn/5-truths-about-the-favor-god

CHAPTER 8: MY ANSWERED PRAYER

One of my most favorite TV shows of all time is A Different World. I loved the main characters, Dwayne Wayne and Whitley Gilbert. I loved the idea of attending a historically black college. I loved the show so much; I decided at age 12 I was going to Hillman College. Yes, H-I-L-L-M-A-N College. I decided to research Hillman, research back when I was 12 was nothing like it is today. Google didn't exist. I don't even think that there were websites where you could go to find out information. The research was looking up information through catalogs and encyclopedias. I spent hours at the library researching Hillman College only to find out that Hillman College did not exist. However, a college known as "Spelman" tweaked my interest. I learned the fictional Hillman College was loosely based on two actual colleges, Spelman in Atlanta, Georgia, and Hampton University in Hampton, Virginia.

I started researching Spelman. I was like, "Oh, it's an all-women college. Okay, I'm going to go. I want to go there." I talked about Spelman all the time when I was in high school. When I got to my senior year, and it was time to apply to schools, there were a lot of programs that told me, "Frenda, we have some schools. Do you want to go to HBCU? It might not be Spelman, because they don't give much financial aid or scholarships. But we can find a HBCU for you." My school counselor and teachers suggested I see a College Counselor at a first-generation college access program, Ada S. McKinley. Based on my GPA, a list of HBCUs that would offer me full-ride scholarships was provided. My test scores weren't the best; however, my GPA was high enough to receive scholarship offers. My mom was not working at the time, so I was also eligible for need-based grants.

The College Counselor we met with that day was so excited when he saw my transcripts. He asked me a few questions about careers. He named a few HBCUs that would love to admit me and offer scholarships. He talked about a college in Ohio, Wilberforce University. He said he could call an admission counselor to get me in and make an offer that day. I smiled and said, "Maybe that school could be my second choice if I don't get admitted to Spelman." Both my mom and the College Counselor stared at me like I was crazy. My mom was a little upset with me. I remember us riding from the Southside back to the Westside on the bus, and she was like, "You mean to tell me that because it's not Spelman you don't want to go? You can go to that school in Ohio for free!"

I looked at my mom and said, "I want to go to Spelman. I've been researching and talking about Spelman since I was 12, remember?" My mom was like, "I understand that, but they are offering you money, and Ohio is not that far from Chicago. At least I can get to you if I need to. Spelman is all the way in Atlanta, and we don't have no family in Georgia." After the Ada S. McKinley experience, I upped my scholarship application completion plans. I went to the library every Saturday morning. I would stay until the library closed. I would research scholarship information, type essays, and mail out completed scholarship application with self-addressed envelopes, because back in the day, that was the only way you could receive a response about the status of your application. I completed over 100 scholarship applications during my senior year. I worked at the James Jordan Boys and Girls Club right up the street from the library. I would go to the library during my breaks. I even competed scholarship applications at work. I knew if I wanted to go Spelman, the only way I would get there was through scholarships and grants.

I was completing scholarship applications but had not received an admissions letter from Spelman. My mom would peek in my room in the middle of the night watching as I wrote essay after essay. There were a few nights she made me go to bed because I went days without sleep; between school, extracurricular activities, my part-time job, and scholarship applications, I was barely getting 2- 3 hours of sleep. I checked the mail every day in anticipation of my admissions letter from Spelman. Every day I would hear school staff say, "You're smart, you really are. You're Crane smart like you're smart in here, but Spelman, I don't know." Every time I would mention Spelman, no one had anything positive to say because they didn't think I was going to be accepted. Teachers would harass me every day, trying to get me to complete applications for other colleges. I think they were trying to look out for me. They wanted me to have a backup plan. My mom was asking me the same questions at home. Out of frustration one day, I yelled out, "Well, if I don't get into Spelman, I'll go to Wilberforce! That's my back up plan! Does that answer satisfy your constant questions?"

One evening I was sitting at the kitchen table working on scholarships when my mom started asking about college. I stopped what I was doing and looked up at her. "Ma, you remember four years ago when I was called out and prophesied to for wearing those yellow shorts? Remember what Prophetess Nina Marie said about me attending the college of my choice. This is my heart's desire; I believe this is where I am supposed to go. I have to trust God." That night, I won my mom over. Her eyes got big. She smiled and said,

"My baby's talking about faith and trusting God. I'm going to trust God with you!" After that night, my mom never said anything negative about Spelman or mentioned another school.

I remember talking to God like every day before I went to sleep and every day when I woke up. I was like, "God?" I would talk to God like I was conversing with someone sitting right in front of me. "I remember the prophecy that you spoke through prophetess Nina Marie, that I will be able to attend the college of my choice, and that I wouldn't have to worry about paying for it, and I would have all the resources I needed to attend. I trust your word. I trust that you spoke through this prophetess to me. I trust that you will take care of me, and I trust that this word will come to pass." I prayed the same prayer every night and every morning for days.

I was home sick with cramps one day. I was alone. My sister Marquitta was at school, and Mom was volunteering in my little sister, Victoria's preschool class. Every time she volunteered, she would take my baby sister, Danyil, with her. If I am not mistaken, Dani wasn't even a year old at the time. I turned on music because worship songs always helped me to relax and sleep, especially when I was sick with cramps. A song by Daryl Coley, "God Is Preparing Me," came on. I had heard the song several times because it was one of my mom's favorite songs, but this particular day, this song made me emotional. It felt like the words from that song were literally penetrating my heart. The words of that song, "God is preparing me for something I cannot handle right now," spoke to my heart. "God is making me ready just because God cares." It was like God was answering my prayers through the words of that song. "God is providing me with what I'll need to carry out the next matter in my life." That day I knew I was going to be offered admissions to Spelman. I knew it and I felt it in my heart. I was just waiting for the physical letter to come in the mail. After that day, instead of saying that same prayer in the morning and at night, I would thank God for my admissions offer.

A week later, in April, I was at work at the Boys & Girls Club. I worked there after school and on some Saturdays. I got a call at work from my mom. When I answered the phone, I could feel the excitement in her voice. "Frenda, you have an envelope from Spelman! It's a big envelope! I'm not going to open it. I want you to open it when you get home." I worked throughout the day with some much excitement. I got home, and my Mom handed me the envelope. I instantly started to cry because I knew it was my acceptance letter. My mom smiled at me with tears in her eyes. She kept saying, "Open it!" I opened the envelope, and the first word I read were, "Congratulations." I wept. My heart was filled with so much gratitude. This was probably the first time in my life in which I believed God for something it happened. All my life, I saw God as my mom's God. If I needed something, I'd tell my Mom, she would pray, and God would answer her. This was the first time I prayed, believed God, and I felt like God answered my prayers.

I returned to school on Monday with my Spelman College acceptance letter in hand. Everyone was so excited, my principal and teachers photo-copied my letter and hung it all around the school. After a week or so of celebrating, people started asking, "That's great that you got in, but how are you going to pay for it?" I honestly was not fazed. I kept reminding myself about the other part of the prophecy, "I was going to have all resources I needed to attend the college of my choice." I felt like I had done my part by applying to over 100 scholarship programs and trusted God to give me favor. Faith without works is dead. My "works" were all the hours and days I put in researching, applying, and writing essays for scholarships. I knew in my heart; God was going to provide the resources. I didn't pray; I thanked God every morning and night each day. At this point, I was living by faith. I convinced my mom to allow me to take the Greyhound bus to Atlanta for the Spelman Experience Weekend event. I saved my money from work to purchase my tickets and to pay the fee for the weekend. I got permission from my principal to be excused from school for three days. I had to travel all day Thursday to make it for the start of the program on a Friday morning. I got back on the bus on Sunday evening in order to get back to Chicago by Monday afternoon.

The first time I stepped on Spelman's campus, I felt my dreams come alive. I knew I was supposed to be there. The Spelman Experience Weekend was beyond amazing. I met some fantastic future Spelmanites. Everyone was so welcoming and encouraging. I went back home on cloud 9. I was a Spelmanite, couldn't no one convince me otherwise. In May, I started receiving responses from scholarship programs. I was awarded a scholarship from the Boys & Girls Club of America for $1,000. I received another scholarship for $5,000 through the Women's Board at the Boys & Girls Club of Chicago. I received several other smaller awards through various organizations. The scholarships were coming in slowly but surely. I was excited for every offer, no matter how large or small. Towards the end of May, my guidance counselor called me to her office. When I walked in, she had the biggest smile on her face. I smiled back, and I was like, "Hey, what's up?" Ms. Deloney started screaming, "You got it! You got it!" I was like, "I got what?" She said, "You got the UNCF scholarship!" She was like, "Oh my God!" She was close to tears, she hugged me, and she was like, "Oh my God!" I nearly cried when I found out the scholarship was a renewable $10,000 a year award! I sat down and counted up all of my scholarship offers, which totaled to about $17,000, which meant I needed approximately $5,000 more to attend Spelman for FREE! I got excited once I remembered I had an interview with the Jackie Robinson Foundation Scholarship committee. The JRF scholarship was for exactly

$5,000. My interview with JRF went well. A couple of weeks later, I found out I didn't get the Jackie Robinson Foundation Scholarship, and I cried.

I dried my tears and told myself, "Maybe there's something else for me. But I felt like JRF was my scholarship." One of the JRF committee members called me personally to let me know that I was a strong candidate. However, JRF only raised a specific amount of money that year for new scholars. He encouraged me to keep working hard and to do exactly what I told the committee I would do whether I received the scholarship or not, "The Jackie Robinson Foundation scholarship would assist me in reaching my goal of attending my dream college. However, if, for some reason, I am not awarded the JRF scholarship, I will somehow have to figure a way to pay the remaining balance. I am willing to do whatever it takes to ensure that my dream comes to total and complete fruition." I received a few smaller scholarships up until graduation day. I worked and saved as much money as I could during the summer.

On Sunday afternoon in July, my mom, sister and I get home after church. We eat and like every other Sunday, we take a good "after church" nap. So we're waking up from our nap. I was downstairs, and my mama was upstairs. The phone rings. I'm like, "Hello?" A familiar voice on the other end of the phone asked, "May I speak with Frenda?" I'm like, "Oh, speaking." The familiar voice began to introduce himself, "Well, you don't remember me? My name is Euclid, from Jackie Robinson Foundation." My heart almost jumped out of my chest. "Yes, I remember you, I do." He says, "How have you been?" I said, "I've been okay." He continues to talk, "Well, how's the scholarship search going?" I said, "I still need a few thousand dollars. But I'm still going to Spelman; I'm going to figure it out." He laughed, and he said, "Is your mom around?" I said, "Yes." He asked, "Well, can she get on the phone with you?" I said, "Hold on," I yelled upstairs, and

I said, "Ma, can you pick up the phone? It's important!" She picks up the phone sounding sleepy and confused, "Yes?"

Mr. Euclid began talking to my mom and I. "Well, let me just say this. I don't know what it is about you but Frenda, you're so different. When you interviewed with us, everybody on the panel loved you. You simply were yourself in the interview. You came in as yourself; you didn't try to be anything or anyone else. You were genuine. You didn't have made-up or rehearsed answers. We enjoyed your interview. Some of the answers you gave us you thought more about how your college education would benefit your family and community, more than you thought about your career or how much money you wanted to make. You are the type of scholar we look for."

I am standing in the middle of the kitchen, holding the phone with tears and snot (sorry TMI) running down my face. He said, "But the issue was we only raised a certain amount, and so we had to cut it down on the number of scholars this year. The panel was so sad about not being able to offer you the JRF scholarship. I do not want to sound creepy, but I would go to bed at night, and I would hear your name." By this time, my mama is in full worship and praise mode. I'm so stuck that I can't even be embarrassed that she's literally speaking in tongues, sobbing and already thanking God before this man could finish. He said, "I would wake up in the morning, and I would hear your name. I'd be going about my day typing on the computer at working, and I would hear your name in the back of my head. I finally got to the point where I'm like, well hell I've got to find some money for this girl because I keep hearing her name.'" I am fighting the deep sobs I can feel in my chest. He's like, "Are you still there?" I managed to whisper, "Yes." Mr. Euclid says, "I'm just calling you to let you know we found money for you. Congratulations, you are the recipient of the 1997 Jackie Robinson Foundation Scholarship Award!" At that point, I could no longer hold in the sobs. I was able to muster a "Thank you."

LIFE/MENTAL HEALTH TIP(S):

Psalm 37:4 (NIV)
Take delight in the Lord, and He will give you the desires of your heart.

<u>DREAM BIG</u>

No matter where you're from, your dreams are valid – *Lupita Nyong'o*

Reality is wrong. Dreams are for real – *Tupac Shakur*

Always remember, you have within you the strength, the patience, and the passion to reach for the stars to change the world – *Harriet Tubman*

The future belongs to those who believe in the beauty of their dreams – *Eleanor Roosevelt*

All our dreams can come true, if we have the courage to pursue them – *Walt Disney*

When you cease to dream. You cease to live – *Malcolm Forbes*

CHAPTER 9:
MY RELATIONSHIP WITH GOD

I entered Spelman College in August of 1997. I was both excited and anxious about my new journey. During my adolescence years, I was pretty much isolated. If I hung out with others, they generally were my sister, Marquitta's friends. Connecting with others was not necessarily easy for me. I was nervous and awkward when it came to friendships and relationships with new people. I was getting used to my college roommate, Kira. Kira was an only child from Connecticut. We spoke over the phone and wrote letters to one another during the summer before we enrolled at Spelman. Kira had a big and bubbly personality. After our first week of Spelman, it seemed like Kira knew everyone. She literally spoke to everyone. I got used to Kira's outgoing personality. However, I was still socially awkward and filled with anxiety.

My anxiety was literally eased in one night. It was the night I connected with my Spelman sisters: Kendrea (Georgia), Jamonica (Alabama), Shayla (Houston), Kira (Connecticut), Allegra (New Jersey), and Tanya (Ohio). We decided to order pizza and eat in the lounge at the end of our hall. We sat and talked all night. We discussed our families, our struggles, our victories, and our goals. I felt so comfortable, safe, and free around this group of women. I felt like I could be myself without any judgments. We talked, we laughed, we cried until the wee hours of the next day. I remember heading back to my room, smiling as I closed my eyes. I had friends. I had sisters. I believe God connected our hearts and lives that night. Cherise (Minnesota) and Andrea (South Carolina) joined the Spelman sister circle later that year. It's been over twenty years later and we are still sisters. We are a family. We recently met up in New York to celebrate, Kendrea's 40th Birthday. We had a fantastic time.

Jamonica just had her second baby girl, so I have two nieces; Princess Jayla & Princess Victoria. Kira couldn't make it to the NYC celebration that September, but I was able to see her in North Carolina in November of last year. I finally met her baby girl Ella (she also has a son, my nephew, Nigel). Cherise is the mommy of 3 amazing kids (Sydney, Devin Jr & Camille). Allegra has a son, Anson Jr.; he's the cutest ever. Andrea just moved from Japan to Italy with her beautiful family, which includes my nephew Jackson & niece Addison. Tanya, the genius of the sister circle, graduated a semester earlier than everyone else. She's the proud mommy of 5 awesome kids (Geoffrey, Joshua, Taylor, Brooke, and Braylen).

My first semester in college seemed to be going well. I was finally getting used to college life, time management, studying, getting to class on time, writing papers, and reading what seemed like every second of the day. I had my sister-friends to support, encourage, and hang out. There was one thing missing, church. I grew up going to church. Sundays were for church. I attended church for a semester or so with one of my professors and her family but after I stopped going to church with them I felt awkward, not attending church on Sundays. So I started attending World Changers in College Park, GA. I was familiar with World Changers because my mother used to watch their broadcast each Sunday. I would get up early each Sunday to take the MARTA (Atlanta's public transportation system) from the Southwest side to the Eastside. I enjoyed the sermons, and the church was huge and beautiful. However, I did not necessarily feel like I was a member of the church because it was so big. I didn't really know anyone, and I didn't have time to join a ministry so I could get to know others. The long commute to get to church for service and then traveling back to campus after service took up my entire Sunday. I would leave campus around 7 am to make it to the 9 am service. I would not get back to campus until about 2 pm. I would eat then sleep until well into the evening. I tried attending small bible study groups during the week, but the commute was stressful, and I would find myself walking from the West end MARTA train station to campus at night. I am from the Westside of Chicago, but this was not a smart decision. Again, I enjoyed the sermons on Sunday, but the commute was a bit too much.

There were churches that sent coach buses to campus to pick up students from Spelman, Morehouse, Clark Atlanta University and Morris Brown College. Most of my sister-friends chose to attend New Birth Missionary Baptist Church. I visited a few times, but I just didn't feel connected. It was lit, though. I enjoyed the music, the sermons, and the church was full of young people. Riding the coach bus to and from church was pretty convenient. However, I didn't feel connected, so I continued to go to World Changers until I found myself missing a Sunday here and there. I looked up one day and realized I had not been to church in a month of Sundays.

Although church attendance was a little spotty, I still made an effort to talk to God and read my Bible daily. I remember praying to God about finding a church where I felt like I belong. I found a place. It was not a church, though. I found my place through a choir. New Life was a college choir made up of students from Spelman College, Morehouse College, Clark Atlanta University, and Morris Brown College. Some of the choir members also attended Georgia Tech, Georgia State, and Emory University. A few of my sister-friends joined the choir, and they loved it. Each week we would sit around the lunch table, and they would talk about New Life Choir. I was intrigued, so I decided to go to one of the choir rehearsals on campus.

I walked in thinking I was just going to sit in the back as a spectator, but I was mistaken. I was asked by one of the choir captains if I was a soprano or alto? I had no clue. I legit cannot sing. Trust me; I have tried. I think Kendrea grabbed my hand and said, "We are altos" and led me to the alto section. Just like that, I became a member of the Atlanta University Center (AUC) New Life choir. I cannot sing but felt connected when I attended Tuesday night choir rehearsals. We learned songs and practiced, but we also prayed, had bible study, and we worshipped until the presence of God entered the room. It was like nothing that I have ever experienced before in my life.

I was finally developing a personal relationship with God. I was learning how to communicate with God through prayer. I was learning the importance of worshipping God. I experienced God on a level of faith when I was in high school when I was praying for favor and blessings, and God answered my prayers. However, I learned to hear the voice of God in my daily life through New Life Choir. Through the choir, I also developed life-long friends. My Morehouse brothers are still my brothers today (Pete, Geoff and Everette). I met one of my best friends, Jasmine (Jazz is also the mother of 2 of my godsons: Tre and Jackson). Jazz attended Clark Atlanta University. I also met my brother, Derrick aka Moose, he attended Clark Atlanta as well. I met my sister, Nikia, through Jazz, although Nikia attended Spelman with me. Jazz and Nikia were both from Connecticut. Nikia and are sisters for life (I am Auntie to her beautiful boys Landon and Levi). I met my sister, Sumaya.

She was a theater major from Ohio. We connected one night at the AUC Block Party and have been sisters ever since. I also met my amazing big sisters through New Life; Tyesha, Nina, Carol (Carol is Jymirah, my first godchild's mother) and the twins, April and Alicia. April and Alicia were literally my angelic big sisters. There were so many times and instances in which they lovingly looked out for me, took care of me when I was sick, fed me when I did not have food to eat and simply loved me without conditions. They will forever have a place in my heart.

I would visit World Changers and New Birth from time to time, but I was not attending church regularly. During this time, I was, however, attending New Life Choir rehearsal every week. About a year or so after joining the choir, the leader of New Life Choir started a church, New Life International Family Church. I remember that first church service like it was yesterday. I joined New Life Church. I had finally found a church where I felt connected, and I felt like I belong. New Life International Family Church is where I learned to use my spiritual gifts to minister to others. I learned how to serve my community and how to share the love of God with others. I would like to take this time to publicly thank Bishop Jeronn Williams and Dr. LaToya Williams (aka Lady, Lady) for not only taking the time to pour into my life but also in the lives of hundreds of other young people who were in search of God. Your labor of love will never go unnoticed.

After I graduated from Spelman College in 2001, I stayed in Atlanta for two years. I worked and enrolled in a master's program at Clark Atlanta University. I could sense that I was supposed to move back home a few times, but I was comfortable in Atlanta. I did miss my family. I missed my mom. I missed my sisters: Marquitta, Victoria, and Danyil. By this time, my sister, Marquitta, had given birth to my niece, Briana Renee. I felt like I was missing my niece grow up.

Although I missed my family, I decided to stay in Atlanta. Then things started happening; life started happening. I applied for a teaching position at a charter school after I left my job at the Study Hall, an after school enrichment program. We picked students up after school, brought them to our program, fed them dinner, and provided homework assistance. We also offered enrichment activities and dropped each student off at their homes after the program ended.

I worked at the Study Hall for a few years and lived in one of the houses on the Study Hall's campus. Now that I think about it, I probably left my position at the Study Hall prematurely. When I left my position at the Study Hall, I had to find a job as well as an apartment. So here I am, in a new apartment and I had to figure out how to pay rent. I worked as a substitute teacher for the charter school when they could not offer me a full-time position. I was also working as a Social Work intern for my master's program. I was not making enough money to keep up with bills and rent. I was always late with my rent.

The apartment manager was still very accommodating, but at the same time, she was like, "Listen, girl, you got to get it together. I cannot keep covering for you." I knew I probably should've just said, "Let me pack up and just go home." That's what I was supposed to do, but I didn't. I ended up getting evicted. I mean, all of my stuff, everything that I owned was thrown away. That was very traumatic for me. I still tried to stay with friends and figure out a plan to get back on my feet, but I finally I was like, "I need to go home." I ended up returning to Chicago during the winter of 2003. I returned home with a suitcase I borrowed and with clothes that were given to me after my eviction. I returned to Chicago, embarrassed, broken, and confused about my future.

LIFE/MENTAL HEALTH TIP(S):

I John 5:14 (NIV)
This is the confidence we have in approaching God: that if we ask anything according to His will, He hears us.

6 Simple Steps To Building A Relationship With God

"How do I build a relationship with God?" is a question I'm often asked, and it's tempting to make the process more complicated than it needs to be.

- **Don't make it complicated!**

If you have a desire to build a relationship with God, that is the essential first step. That sets your intention and focus. The rest is a matter of taking regular baby steps towards God and being open to what happens. If you want to build a relationship with God, you have to go, metaphorically, to where God is and place yourself in His presence. Only in that way can you receive the gifts He wants to give you.

- **God is always present but never pushy**

God is not going to knock you over to get closer to you. We have the freedom to invite Him into our lives or not. You're not likely to wake up one morning with the certain feeling that you've become friends with God (though that could happen). Like human relationships, it usually takes an investment of time and attention and caring, and it's up to you to take the initiative of moving closer to God—of placing yourself in His presence and just abiding there. It's rarely dramatic. You might not even feel anything at all at first. But when you do this over and over again, the emotion and belief will follow, and you'll begin to trust He is with you and is guiding you.

- **Keep it simple**

Don't make this hard, keep it simple. Think of building a relationship with God just as you would a relationship with anyone else. Suppose you wanted to get to know a certain person better. The way you would do that is the way you can approach your relationship with God:

1. **Take the time to touch bases with God,** acknowledging and giving thanks for His presence.
2. **Invite Him to come close** — to sit with you at your heart's kitchen table and just hang out.
3. **Talk:** Some days this will feel like pouring out your heart. Other days, it will be casual chit-chat. Occasionally, all you'll be able to manage is, "Here I am, Lord. Please be with me." Between friends, it's all good.
4. **Listen:** Remember to make it a two-way conversation and expect to hear from God, just as you would from a trusted friend. God wants you to know how much He loves you. He wants to offer support and guidance to you. If you don't take the time to listen, you won't hear His "still, small voice." For me, this communication from God comes in any of various forms: thoughts, feelings, music, reading, nature, other people, or circumstances. Sometimes I only recognize God's voice in retrospect.
5. **Make contact throughout your day.** Being in touch with God doesn't have to be only during times of meditation or prayer. It can be while you're on the run, when you're in the midst of activities, or when you have a moment's break.
6. **Take action when you hear God's voice.** If you feel God is guiding you or telling you something, take action on it as soon as possible. The insight you receive may only show you where to take the next step, but once you've taken that step, the following

step will appear in front of you. Even though there is electrical power in your house, the light doesn't turn on until you have flipped the switch to harness that power. God's power is waiting for you to remember to flip the switch.

Make these six steps regular practices, and expect it to take time. You'll find yourself gradually learning to recognize God's voice and beginning to trust it. One day, you'll realize you're in a relationship with God that is treasured and invaluable in your life. Don't confuse the emotion with the reality. Even with earthly friends, some days you feel closer to them than others.

Reference:

https://www.heartspoken.com/6246/6-simple-steps-to-building-a-relationship-with-god/

CHAPTER 10: MY 21ST BIRTHDAY

When I celebrated my 21st birthday, I was in my senior year at Spelman anticipating graduation that May. I was living in an apartment building near campus. Although it was an apartment off-campus, it was an apartment building that catered specifically to college students. We did not pay rent monthly, we paid rent each semester similar to the way we paid for room and board when I lived on my college campus. I was using my college refund checks (scholarship and grant money I had left over after paying tuition and fees to Spelman) to pay for rent, bills, and for food. I was also working part-time at the Study Hall.

I invited all my friends over on my birthday. I had about 30 friends over. My friend, Elgin, was a student at Morehouse. As a gift, Elgin cooked dinner for me and all of my friends. Elgin was a fantastic cook. We were having a blast, singing, watching TV, listening to music, playing games, and eating all of Elgin's great food. After dinner, things shifted a bit. Everyone decided to speak words of affirmation over me. I was overwhelmed by the positive words of encouragement and affirmation from my friends. My best friend, Jazz, started singing. Jazz is not only an amazing singer; she is an anointed psalmist. When she sings, she invokes the presence of God. So here we are, thirty young adults in my one bedroom apartment; hands lifted and worshipping God.

Everyone seemed to be worshipping in their own way. Some

were off in corners worshiping, some were lying on the floor, some were sitting on couches and chairs, and some were facing the wall as they prayed. Y'all, we were so deep! When I tell you, we were saved like seriously saved. We were a bit immature and naive about some things, but we wanted God. I was sitting on the floor, with my hands lifted and eyes closed. I remember weeping because I was so grateful to see another birthday. I could feel God's presence and love for me. Then I heard God say, "A lot of your friends are going to get married very young, right after college. Although many of your friends are going to get married, you will not marry young. I need you to be okay with this."

I promise you as God as my witness, I heard those words clear as day. "I need you to be okay with this because there are some things that I need to do in your life, I need to do some things within you before you're ready for marriage. I need you to trust that I have your best interest in mind. I need you to trust my will for your life." It was like God was sitting right next to me on that floor, whispering in my ear. I heard God say a few times, "I need you to be okay with this." I responded, "Lord, whatever your will is from my life, I surrender to it. Help me to be okay with it." I may have cried myself to sleep right there on that floor. Now, I didn't know that I was going to be 40 years old and still not married LOL. God didn't give me an age range or any specifics. I probably should have asked.

Many of my friends were getting married right after college, and some right after finishing graduate school. People were getting married left and right. I was good for the most part. I had accepted the fact that I was not getting married any time soon, and I was focused on my education and career. I was working on a 2nd master's degree while working as a high school counselor for Chicago Public Schools. I was traveling the word with my sister-chicks (I met some amazing women via a chat room and fan club in 2003. We immediately become sisters. Valencia, Barbara, Bianca, Wendy, Tracy, Janice, Tina. PJ, Sheree, Nicole and several other sister-chicks travelled around the country as well as internationally for the past 15 years.) I was busy focusing on my personal healing, deliverance, career, education, ministry, family, friends and being a godmother. I did not have time to think about marriage and children. Then it happened. I turned 28.

I don't know what it was about turning 28 that triggered me. I found myself feeling like I was over the single life. I wanted marriage, but more than anything, I wanted children (I had godchildren, but I wanted biological children). I remember praying to God like, "Oh, okay. So how much longer do I have to wait?" I felt in my heart that after seven years, surely it was about that time. I remember year 28 being a very rough year for me. I spent seven years working on issues of identity, healing from father wounds, getting delivered and restored from the molestation, and I could feel my life changing, but it was not changing fast enough. I wanted so badly to quicken my healing, deliverance, and restoration process. So many people around me were married and starting families. Here I was still dealing with mental, emotional, and spiritual issues and struggles. I was tired of fighting and working out my soul salvation. I was angry. I was angry about the things that happened to me. I was angry about the things I could not control. I was angry about the time and energy it was taking to feel whole and healed. I was angry about the curse, I mean the word God spoke over me at age 21. I was over it!

LIFE/MENTAL HEALTH TIP(S):

Isaiah 40:31
But they that wait upon the Lord shall renew their strength; they shall mount up with the wings as eagles; they shall run, and not be weary; and they shall walk, and not faint.

10 Things to Do While You're Waiting on God

Perhaps this is why the Bible talks so much about waiting.
God wants us to know that waiting is far from a passive
activity in which we do nothing. In fact, Scripture teaches us
that God wants us to actively participate in the work he
desires to accomplish. Waiting strategically can cultivate good
fruit in in our lives such as patience, perseverance, and
endurance. It also draws us closer to our Savior and points
those who are watching us to the gospel.

Here are 10 things to do while you wait:

1. Believe that the God who saved you hears your
cries (Micah 7:7).
2. Watch with expectancy, but be prepared for unexpected
answers (Psalm 5:3).
3. Put your hope in his Word (Psalm 130:5-6).
4. Trust in the Lord, not in your own understanding
(Proverbs 3:5-6).
5. Resist fretting, refrain from anger, be still, and choose
patience (Psalm 37:7-8).
6. Be strong and take courage (Psalm 27:13-14; 31:24).
7. See it as an opportunity to experience God's goodness
(Psalm 27:13; Lamentations 3:25).
8. Wait for God's promise instead of going your own way
(Acts 1:4).
9. Continue steadfastly in prayer, being watchful with
thanksgiving (Colossians 4:2).
10. Remember the blessings yet to come (Isaiah 30:18).

"Be still before the Lord and wait patiently for him; those
who wait for the Lord shall inherit the land; But for you, O
Lord, do I wait; it is you, O Lord my God, who will
answer." Christ is the answer! He is your rest and the treasure

you seek. Wait for the Lord.

Reference:

https://unlockingthebible.org/2017/08/what-to-do-while-youre-waiting-on-god/

CHAPTER 11: MY SOUL TIE

I think year 28 was challenging because I found myself comparing my life with the lives of others. I was paying entirely too much attention to the relationships of the women around me. Many of my friends and co-workers were either married, engaged, or dating. Honestly, I was silently dealing with loneliness. My friends would try to get me to go on dates, but I would always decline. If I was not attracted to a guy or if I could not see a future with a guy, I felt like it would be a waste of time and energy to go out on a date with him. I didn't believe in dating just to date. I didn't believe in wasting my time nor the time of others. So, if I didn't like you, why would I go on a date with you? So that I can have a free meal? For companionship? Nah. I didn't believe in leading people on. I didn't judge people who like to go on random dates, that just wasn't for me. Some of my friends would be like, "Oh, I'm going to go out with this guy." I'd be like, "Well, what do you like about him?" They would say "Nothing really. I'm going to get this free meal real quick, though," or "I want to just go out on a date just to go because I haven't been out in a while." I didn't judge them, leading people on was just not my thing.

Just like I did not understand how or why my friends and colleagues would randomly date guy; they couldn't understand why I was waiting for marriage to have sex. When I was in high school, I didn't feel pressured to have sex. I was too focused on my studies and was in my own world.

However, I experienced much peer-pressure in my adult years. The thought of having sex with someone I did not love or who was not committed to me via marriage, scared me. I felt like if I had sex, something terrible would happen like I would end up pregnant the first time I did something or I'd end up with an incurable disease (let me pause here to say, I think children are gifts and blessings no matter how they get here). I always felt like I couldn't get away with stuff that others could. I would always get caught. So, that was always in the back of my mind. I wasn't necessarily like, "Oh, I'm not having sex before marriage," because I was trying to be holy, even though that's the point of it. The Bible does say, "Be Holy because I am Holy." I was doing it because that's what I was taught to do, and I felt like if I held on to my virginity, I could protect myself: my heart, my spirit, my life. I was legit afraid of heart break.

Molestation is a gateway to lust and perversion. I struggled with lust and perversion all through adolescence and my young adult years. I was a virgin, but I was reading trashy romance novels full of graphic and sexual content. I would watch erotic movies with explicit sex scenes. I would read and watch erotic books and movies, and after I would struggle with feelings of guilt, shame, and condemnation. In my heart and mind, I was dirty. I think I used my virginity to help me cope with the negative thoughts I had about myself. I was mentally tormented. I remember praying to God like, "I'm trying to save myself from marriage, but I need to hurry up and get married because I don't think I can do this any longer." I thought getting married would help me rid myself of my issues with lust and perversion. I was ignorant. I wasn't even educated on the subject of virginity. I was just doing it for religious purposes, and to make myself feel better for my dirty thoughts.

As stated before, year 28 was tough for me because I was getting closer and closer to age 30. I remember saying to

God, "Okay. I'm almost 30. I know you said I wasn't getting married young, 30 is not young." I was so irritated because I felt like God was ignoring me. Amid my sexual frustrations, I randomly met a guy. I took my students to Malcolm X College for a college expo. I guess he was there with his students also. I was in line; he was behind me, and he started talking to me. I smiled and answered his questions with one-word answers. I tried to ignore him nicely, but he kept talking. He kept pressing me to talk to him. I finally stop fighting it and let my guard down.

We introduced ourselves. He was a high school Literature teacher. He made me laugh. We were talking about our students and why we chose the field of education as a career. We finally made it to the front of the lunch line. I grabbed my food and went to sit down to eat. He followed me to my table. I was like, "You don't have to sit with your students?" He responded, "Wow, you not sitting with yours." I pointed to the tables behind me. My students were sitting eating lunch. They were pointing a whispering to each other, "Look at Ms. Rodgers trying to get boo'ed up." I gave them a quick, "don't play with me glance" and they stopped whispering. He pointed at the tables in front of us. "Mine sitting right here." He looked in the direction of his students. We talked until the end of the expo. When he asked for my number, I gave it to him with no hesitation. He was probably the third guy I had ever given my number to. In college, I gave my dorm room phone number to 2 guys, one my freshmen year and the other during my sophomore year. When guys would ask for my number, I would decline. If they would not take "no" for an answer, I would give them wrong numbers. I know, that was bogus.

I never spoke to the first guy because I did not answer my phone for two weeks after I gave him my number. I was so weird. I actually went out on a date with the second guy. He was my co-worker. I worked at one of the Boys & Girls

Clubs in Atlanta. He was a nice guy, but I wasn't attracted to him. He looked like a thug with his gold teeth and saggy jeans, but he wasn't. He was far from it. I mean, he was from the "streets" but he was educated, he had never been in trouble with the law and he was so loving and sweet towards me. I just wasn't attracted to him. He kept asking me out for months, so I finally agreed to go out with him. We went to the movies and dinner. We had a good time. He walked me back to my dorm, but security wouldn't let him past the gate. I turned to thank him for the movie and dinner, and he hugged me. Every day at work, he pleaded with me to go out with him again. I lied and told him I had a boyfriend back in Chicago. I felt terrible for lying and hurting his feeling because he was a nice guy. I just wasn't attracted to him.

I gave the Literature teacher my number. By the time we got back on the school bus to head back to school, he was calling my phone. "It was nice meeting you today. I am looking forward to getting to know you. Can we meet up to talk some more?" We ended up meeting at Barnes & Noble downtown later that week. We talked for hours until the bookstore closed. We decided to go to dinner. We said our goodbyes at the "red line" train station. He asked me to give him a call when I got home. I called him as soon as I walked into my apartment. We talked until we fell asleep. We spoke every day over the phone. We added each other on Myspace. I think Facebook was super new. There was no Instagram or Twitter. Myspace was the place. The high school I worked at wasn't far from his school. He worked at a high school on the Westside. After work, we would just hang out. When we would go eat, we took turns paying the bill. We were getting to know each other, but we never put a name or title on what we were doing. That was a huge mistake. You never go into any kind of relationship, without defining it. But we were talking every night and going out almost every day. He worked with the youth at his church. I was the youth leader at my church. We had a lot in common. Sometimes he'd be like,

"Come visit my church," and I would invite him to mine, but we never visited each other's church.

He was a nice guy, and although we were spending a lot of time together, I still didn't know him. I brought him around my friends, and my sisters met him. He talked a lot about his family and friends, but I never met any of them. Well, I met one of his sisters by accident. We were at Dave & Buster's playing games, and his sister was there with her husband. She spotted us and walked over like, "Hi." He seemed nervous, he was like, "Oh, this is my friend, Frenda." She looked me up and down and was like, "Hey." She looked me right in my eyes, then looked at him, "Where is such and such?" I forget the name of the girl she asked about, but he clearly knew who she was referring to because he cut her off quickly and grabbed my hand to walk away. I called him when I got home that night. I was so agitated. "Okay, what are we doing? If you call me, and I don't answer my phone, you have an attitude. You are always asking me to check in with you every day. When I don't, you get mad. We hang out almost every day. What are we doing? Are we just friends?" He was silent. I asked her about the girl his sister mentioned. I was like, "I'm sure I don't have a right to know this because we're not in a relationship, but who is this girl? You are with me all the time." He was like, "Oh, that's my ex. I was with her for a long time. We broke up. We have a history of breaking up and making up. My sister is just used to her because I've been with her for so long." So I'm like, "Well, how do you feel about her?" He responded, "It's over between us."

I kind of pulled back some after that. We still talked on the phone and hung out from time to time, but not every day. One day we were talking, and the subject of sex came up. I was forced to tell him I was a virgin. He played it off well. I could see it on his face, like, "What?" I don't feel like he ever pressured me to do anything, but I knew after I told him "my secret" that we weren't going to be as close in friendship as we had been. I just knew it.

We continued with our untitled situation-ship. We were both easily irritated and frustrated with each other. One day we got into an argument over the phone. He hung up and did not call or text me for weeks. I called and texted him daily. Now that I think about it, I may have slightly stalked him. My feelings were hurt. I didn't know what was going on. I didn't know that you can have a soul tie with somebody even if you never kissed or had sex with them. So, that's what I developed in this situation-ship, a soul tie. He finally, after a couple of weeks called me and apologized for how he acted. He was just saying, "He getting frustrated with our relationship." I asked him, "What relationship? Because we never defined what we were doing." We started back talking, and by this time, Facebook was popular. It was his birthday; I took him to dinner. We had a good time. No arguments, it was a good day. That night I wished him a happy birthday on his Facebook page, and he deleted it. I was pissed. I called and texted him; he did not respond.

When he finally returned my call, I flipped out. "Why did you delete the birthday message that I sent to you? I thought we were over whatever you were mad about." He was like, "Oh, I wasn't mad. I just delete messages off my page. I don't leave the birthday messages on my page." I'm like, "That doesn't make sense. It's your birthday." He said, "I just don't." I was like, "Well, there's birthday messages on your page right now." He was like, "Oh, I'm about to go delete them now." I was so frustrated. "Your birthday was two weeks ago." I was over it. I told him, "Listen, you're a cool dude, and I know we claim we are just friends. But what we're doing has gone beyond friendship. I think at this point, if we're not going to pursue a relationship, let's just move on. More power to you. I wish you the best." He started yelling, "What are you talking about?" I asked him to calm down, but he kept yelling, so I hung up the phone. I texted him and told him to have a nice life. He texted me back, saying he wasn't going anywhere, and I better answer my phone. I turned my phone off and cried myself to sleep.

He would text me and send me messages via Facebook. I deleted his number from my phone and off of Facebook. He would then send messages through my sister, Marquitta, or my co-workers, but I ignored him. The final straw was him sending me a long email. I responded to him and asked him nicely to leave me alone because he did not want to be with me. No, we cannot be friends; we did not know how to be friends. I tried to get over him by going out with a guy one of my friends introduced me to. The new guy was nice and attractive, but my heart was still tied to the other guy. I went out a few more times with the new guy, but it didn't last. I honestly never gave the new guy a chance.

My "friend" ended up marrying his ex-girlfriend. I had developed a soul tie with this guy. We never kissed, we never held hands, but I opened my heart and life to him. It took some time, but I prayed and asked God to help me get over him. I asked God to help me not to be bitter and unforgiving because, honestly, I could not find fault with him. I entered that situation-ship without defining it. I let my guard down and did not put up boundaries. I asked God to help me to forgive myself.

LIFE/MENTAL HEALTH TIP(S):

Galatians 5:1 (ESV)
For freedom Christ has set us free; stand firm therefore, and do not submit again to a yoke of slavery.

How to Break a Soul Tie

A Soul Tie is such an intimate and close connection where you bond so much with another person, place, object, idea, etc. that it can't escape your mind. Daily interactions are just a sliver of the powerful bonding that occurs in a Soul Tie. Usually, you can visualize in your head two ghostly vessels tied by a cord. The distance between them is only as far away as their hearts and minds. A Soul Tie can feel like it can never be rubbed off. Here are five ways to break a Soul Tie.

- Start to exercise:

Investing in yourself helps build confidence. When you start to see the belly fat reduce, or that your arms are getting a little stronger, you can become mindful. When you work out, DO NOT do this to get back together with your Soul Tie. Invest in yourself for you.

- Learn about your attachment style (and how to heal it):

There are three attachment types: Anxious, Secure, and Avoidant. When we get scared or triggered by childhood traumas, these styles come out. Securely attached people generally had a healthy childhood and are better at approaching intimate relationships. Anxious and avoidant people find intimacy more of a struggle. This is often because of a trauma in early life, such as neglect, poor parenting, or an abusive relationship. By doing healing work, and joining an organization that supports you in this, you can do work on yourself to heal better from your Soul Tie ending.

- Continue your spiritual journey.

Use the Bible App to search scriptures on Anxiety, Fear, Trust, and Peace to help you deal with grief and loss from your Soul Tie and other friendships ending.

- Take "you" time (that makes you feel good).

Does reading that novel bring a smile to your face? How about talking about that Captain Marvel movie that you saw with your friend? Taking some space in silence? Or going to the park with your dog? Feeling good for once, and not thinking about the ways that your Soul Tie hurt you, is a great way to make yourself feel more like that superhero, recharging your powers!

- Seek a mental health professional.

See a counselor/therapist. Going to College Counseling is FREE. And if you are not in college, you can use hotlines, crisis text lines, mentors, someone with training and gentle support to help. Losing a Soul Tie is like losing a close loved one. You deny, and you want to pretend like they will come back if only. But it is so important that with any impulse to reach out to your Soul Tie, you reach out to a mental health professional instead.

Reference:

https://vocal.media/humans/how-to-break-a-soul-tie

CHAPTER 12: PORN ADDICTION

When I returned back to Chicago after living in Atlanta for 7 years, I was looking for a church. I was back visiting the church I grew up in with my mom on Sundays, but here I was again, not feeling connected. My mom and I heard about a Purity Conference hosted by Prophetess Nina Marie Leslie (the prophetess who prophesied to me when I was 13). My mom and I registered for the conference. I was excited about the conference because I was still struggling with lust and perversion. I was hoping someone could give me some pointers on staying pure in mind and body because the struggle was real. I was legit trying to figure out a way not to think about sex. But the truth of the matter is: I'm a female; I'm a woman; I'm a sexual being. So, I'm going to think about sex. It's normal to think about sex.

We attended the Purity Conference. My mom and I greeted Prophetess Nina Marie when she entered the room. I stayed connected with her via phone and mail once I entered college. I would send her postcards and letters from college with my grades every time one of her prophetic words came to pass. I also made sure I attended some of her conferences when I was in town. We were building a friendship, somewhat of a mentor/mentee relationship. There was a preacher by the name of Matthew Stevenson who spoke at the conference. He was so young. He was like 18 or 19 years old. However, he was hands down the best speaker and preacher at the conference. He said he was a pastor at a church called World Deliverance, located on 38th and Michigan. Services were held in the afternoons on Sundays. My sister and I went to that 38th & Michigan location a few times, but never when World Deliverance was in service. We either showed up too late or too early.

We decided to try to visit the church one last time. When we drove up, we noticed cars parked on the side of the building. We got out of the car and walked into the church. As we entered the church, a little girl (Oni Devine) around three years old greeted us at the door, "Welcome to World Deliverance." We finally found it. Long story short, we were connected the first day we visited. We visited a couple more times, then joined. There were less than 50 members at the church at that time. After we joined, several members attended the church's annual leadership retreat. We were invited to attend but due to our work schedules we could not. Upon returning from the leadership retreat, we learned that the name of the church was changed to the International Church of Fire.

I joined World Deliverance/International Church of Fire (currently known as All Nations Worship Assembly) during one of the darkest times of my life. I truly believe if I had not found and joined my life to All Nations Worship Assembly, my life would have spiraled out of control. I was still on my journey towards wholeness through healing, deliverance, and restoration. The fight for healing is hard. Yes, God was with me. Yes, I had some fantastic leaders who supported me. Yes, I had my sisters, sister-chicks and friends fighting with me. It was still so hard and draining. My church needed a Youth Leader. Although I loved young people (I was a high school counselor and was over the youth at my former church), I did not think I was worthy to lead them. My struggles with pervasion and lust intensified. I was now secretly watching porn. Now, let me pause here to say, I am not sharing my struggles with porn addiction to judge anyone. I know people who do not see anything wrong with watching porn. I am not here to argue if watching porn is right or wrong. This is not the point of sharing my story. I am sharing my story so all can see the negative results of any addiction. Addiction ruin lives!

I chose to struggle in isolation because I was embarrassed. Here I was leading young people in my church, and I was struggling with lust, perversion, and porn. I would busy my life around the young people I was serving to take my mind off of my struggles. This will sometimes help because when I was busy serving others, I did not have time to focus on myself. I would go months without watching porn or having perverse thoughts, just to slip right back into old habits of my struggle. Although I was struggling in my heart, mind, and soul, serving those young men and women gave me life. They loved me, unconditionally. They appreciated me in a way that I had never felt appreciated before. They honored me for the time I spent investing in them, listening to them without judgment, and loving them without restraint.

I tried several times to leave my position as Youth Leader because of my struggles with lust, perversion, and porn. People from the outside looking in were like, "Oh, Frenda, you're great for the youth because they love you. You understand them. You are a role model because you're a virgin." I would just sit there feeling like, "A virgin that is addicted to porn. Right. If y'all only knew." Once I realized my Apostle was not going to allow me to abandon my position as Youth Leader (he believed in me and he refused to allow me to give up on myself), I started to think of ways to better serve the young people in my life. Many of the youth were dealing with relationship issues with friends. Many of them asked about advice as it related to dating. I thought about how I did not have anyone to openly discuss topics like this when I was younger. I decided to develop a curriculum specifically for my youth that focused on dating, sex, pregnancy, STDs, contraceptives, abstinence, and celibacy.

I scheduled a meeting with my Apostle to discuss the program/curriculum. I felt like just teaching abstinence was not enough. I needed to have open and honest conversations with them about sex. Because in my mind, I'm like, "I need to save them for the struggle that I'm dealing with." No one openly discussed the topic of sex with me. I was told just don't do it. Young people are told, don't do it with no explanation. Then they are left to try to figure things on their own. At the end of the program, the youth would take a vow of celibacy or virginity. My Apostle gave me his full support. There were a few parents who chose not to allow their teens to participate after they saw the curriculum. They were like, "That's something that I want to discuss with my child personally." I understood. Then there were other parents who could not wait to sign their youth up.

The eight-week sessions went well. The youth trusted me enough to have honest and open conversations after I promised each of them; I would not disclose any information shared to anyone, including their parents. I also went over rules with the group each session; the number one rule being, what was discussed in the group stayed in the group. No one was allowed to repeat any information they heard in the group with anyone, including their parents. Parents were told the same rules. If any youth broke this rule, they would be asked not to return to the group. Although the sessions were going well, I was battling daily headaches and sicknesses through the entire program. I rarely get migraines, but during this time, I got migraines weekly. I fought through it and made sure I was present for the youth each week.

My apostles allowed me to conduct the commitment ceremony on a Sunday in front of the church. Each youth was given a ring to wear around their neck (on a chain) and a certificate of completion after we publicly made vows of sexual purity and celibacy. I think the program was a good experience for them; I just don't think it was enough. They needed an open forum to discuss issues regularly. I was not able to provide consistent discipleship for each of them because I was one person, and I was honestly still feeling like I was unworthy to teach or assist with anything related to sexual purity. In my eyes, although I was physically a virgin, I did not feel like I was sexually pure.

LIFE/MENTAL HEALTH TIP(S):

I Corinthians 10:13-14 (NIV)
No temptation has overtaken you, except what is common to mankind. And God is faithful; he will not let you be tempted beyond what you can bear. But when you are tempted, he will also provide a way out so that you can endure it. Therefore, my dear friends, flee from idolatry.

ADDICTION
Although "porn addiction" isn't an official diagnosis recognized by the American Psychiatric Association (APA); experiencing an uncontrollable compulsion to view porn can be as problematic for some people as other behavioral addictions.

What does addiction look like?
Simply viewing or enjoying porn doesn't make you addicted to it, nor does it require fixing.
On the other hand, addictions are about lack of control — and that can cause significant problems.

Your viewing habits may be a cause for concern if you:

- find that the amount of time you spend watching porn keeps growing
- feel as though you need a porn "fix" — and that fix gives you a "high"

95

- feel guilty about the consequences of viewing porn
- spend hours on end perusing online porn sites, even if it means neglecting responsibilities or sleep
- insist that your romantic or sexual partner views porn or acts out porn fantasies even though they don't want to
- are unable to enjoy sex without first viewing porn
- are unable to resist porn even though it's disrupting your life

Can you stop on your own or should you see a professional?

You may be able to gain control over your porn viewing on your own. Here are a few things you can try:
- Delete electronic porn and bookmarks on all your devices.
- Discard all your hard-copy porn.
- Have someone else install anti-porn software on your electronic devices without giving you the password.
- Have a plan — choose another activity or two that you can turn to when that powerful urge hits.
- When you want to view porn, remind yourself how it has affected your life — write it down if that helps.
- Consider if there are any triggers and try to avoid them.
- Partner up with someone else who will ask about your porn habit and hold you accountable.

Keep a journal to track setbacks, reminders, and alternate activities that work.

What treatment options are available?
If you can, consider seeing a therapist to discuss your concerns. They can come up with an individualized treatment plan to help you work through them.

Therapy

Counseling sessions will help you understand what caused the compulsion in the first place. Your therapist can help you develop effective coping mechanisms to change your relationship with pornographic materials.

Support groups

Many people find strength in talking to others who have firsthand experience with the same issue. Ask a primary care physician, mental health professional, or local hospital for information on pornography or sexual addiction support groups

Medication

Treatment for behavioral addictions generally involves talk therapy and cognitive behavioral therapy. But your doctor may recommend medication if you have co-existing conditions, such as depression or OCD.

Reference:

https://www.healthline.com/health/pornography-addiction

CHAPTER 13: MY VIRGINITY

What is a virgin? The term virginity describes someone who has never had sex. This definition is a bit ambiguous. Does oral sex count? What about a woman who has only had sex with another woman? What about masturbation? Is a woman who has experienced forced intercourse or rape no longer considered a virgin? Okay, now that I have your attention, let's talk.

My initial vow to remain a virgin until marriage occurred when I was about twelve years. I was told all my life to save myself for marriage from people who did not save themselves for marriage. How ironic? No shade to anyone but my parents were not married when I was conceived or born. I know more people who were born out of wedlock than I do who were conceived and born within a marriage. I said all of that to say; I think it is time to start having open and honest conversations about what virginity really means and why we (society, the church, families) force the standard of purity down the throat of girls and young ladies while excusing boys and young men from that same standard? One of the reasons why I decided to write this book was to deal with some of the myths, and blatant lies told about virginity. There are millions of virgins around the world. Each person has their own story. I can only tell my story. I DO NOT speak on the behalf of all virgins. I am writing from my personal perspective and experience.

When I made my vow to God to remain a virgin until

marriage, it was heartfelt. I was told in Sunday school, staying a virgin was a commandment from God. I remember going home and searching the bible for that commandment. I could not find it. Virginity is not mentioned at all in the Ten Commandments. I was also told as a young girl that if I kissed a guy, I would get pregnant. I believed this for a long time. One of the biggest lies I was told was if I remain a virgin, God will give me the gift of a great husband. Now don't get me wrong; I know I will be blessed with a great husband one day. But God NEVER told me, my gift for maintaining my virginity would be a husband. I talk to God a lot, every day, several times a day. I have heard others say it, preach it and declare it, but it's simply not true.

I know women who have been blessed with awesome husbands and partners, and they were not virgins when they got married. So to believe that the point of remaining a virgin until marriage is to be given the gift of a husband, is ludicrous. Y'all, I believed the lie. When I turned 36, and I had not received my prize, my reward, my husband, baby, I was pissed! I was angry with God. I was bitter about my journey. It was not until one day; I angrily cried out to God. I was trying to figure out what I did or did not do to cause God not to bless me. I started blaming myself for my struggles with lust, perversion, and porn. Yep, that had to be it. That had to be the reason why God had not blessed me with a husband.

I cried for hours. After I finished screaming, crying, and throwing a tantrum, I promise I heard God say, "Are you done?" I am not really sure how God speak to others, but that is definitely how God communicate with me. God is generally blunt and straight forward when He communicates with me. It may be that way because I am generally direct with I communicate. That same night I received a new level of healing, deliverance, restoration, and revelation that shifted my heart and my life. To make a long story short, I did not sleep at all that night. I sat in the presence of God and allowed my mind, heart, intentions, and motives to be purified. That night I sat and confronted the lies that were told to me as well as the lies I told myself. I asked myself some tough questions: What if I never get married? What if I never have biological children? Would I still serve God? Would I still serve others? Would I still be able to work towards fulfilling my purpose in life? I told God that as much as I wanted to say YES to the latter questions, it was hard for me. I wanted my answer to be YES, but I needed help. I needed GRACE.

I know you are probably wondering, why are you still choosing to remain a virgin? I hate to get technical, but everyone knows sexual intercourse is more than a physical act. Whenever two bodies engage in sex, their souls are also united. I have not yet been introduced to the man that will love me, be committed to me, and is worthy of not only my body and virginity but also my soul. Simply put, I am the gift. I am the prize. I do not regret my decision to remain a virgin until marriage in the least bit. I am not embarrassed about my decision, and I make no apologies for my choice. I also choose to remain a virgin until marriage because the bible does in fact instruct us (men and women) to do so. Don't just take my word for it, go read and study it for yourself (Hebrews 13:4; Thessalonians 4:3-8;
I Corinthians 7:8-9; Genesis 2:24; I Corinthians 6:18-20; Exodus 22:6-17; Romans 12:1-2; Ephesians 5:1-33; Galatians 5:19-21).

Is this virginity lifestyle hard? H E double hockey sticks YES!!! Well, for me it is. I have spoken to a few who feels like virginity has not been hard for them. I take it one day at a time. The older I get, the harder it seems to get. I daily ask for God's grace. I have to be careful about what I watch and read sometimes. I also have to sign off social media from time to time because all you see are couples, families, babies, etc.

Although I am genuinely happy when I see others happy, there are times when emotionally and mentally, I need a break. In regards to dating (yes, I do actively go on dates. I still do not go on casual dates though, don't think I will ever be okay with dating just to date). I have personal boundaries: I do not go on dates after a particular time at night. I do not talk on the phone with someone I am attracted to after 10 pm (there have been a few exceptions to this rule). I only go on dates in public places; I do not accept invites to homes or places in which I am alone.

I have learned to embrace my journey, to embrace who I am, what I've been through, and what I am called to do and be. When people find out I am a virgin, and I am 40 years old, they are like, "What is wrong with you? Are you crazy? Something has to be wrong with you. Are you even attracted to me? Do you have a disease or something?" I promise, I have been asked every one of those questions. I tell people all the time, in high school, I didn't feel the pressure of being a virgin. I didn't feel peer pressure to do certain things. I was so isolated; I didn't care what the next person was doing. It wasn't until my thirties, probably mid-thirties, that I felt the most peer pressure from people who I know loved me, and they didn't mean any harm, but they just could not understand why I was still a virgin. They would say, "You sitting around waiting for sex. You know he's not. Ain't no man waiting to have sex!" This a false statement, I actually personally know a few who are. "What's the point of you waiting so long?" I found myself trying to explain that I did not know I was going to still not be married at 40 years old. My vow to God at age 12 was to remain a virgin until marriage so that means if I am 50 years old (Jesus, please be a present help!) and I am still not married, I will still be a virgin. Period!

I have learned not to judge others. I have friends from all walks of life. I have friends that have a new dude every month. That's their life. I'm not there to judge. If they ask my opinion, I'll give it, and vice versa. But I've had some folks say some stuff to me that I'm like, "I know you want the best for me, but that hurt. That's hurtful what you just said to me, like, 'I don't know what you're waiting for. He's not waiting. What's the purpose of it? You're stupid. You think that you're going to find this guy who's going to wait for you, wait to have sex with you, and then what if you get married and don't even like it?'" I'm saying to myself, "Listen. The only thing I know about sex is what I read about or what I watched. I don't know what that feels like. So even if he is the crappiest person in bed. He's going to be great to me because I don't know what it feels like. I don't have anything to compare with." Honestly, the opinions of others as it relates to my virginity does not really matter to me. If they mattered, I would have never had the courage to write this book.

Do I rack my brain about the stuff I mentioned above? No. I would lose my mind over-thinking. At this point, all I can do is embrace who I am. I am a late bloomer. I just am. I did not learn how to walk until after I was two years old. So that earliest memory I mentioned in the first chapter was probably my second birthday, and I was on that couch because I couldn't walk. I did not get my driver's license until I was 26 years old. I know. Isn't it crazy? 26 years old. I took driver's education in high school but I had no one to take me and teach me how to drive. Then I went to school in Atlanta. I lived there for seven years and never attempted to obtain a license. When I moved back to Chicago, I took the bus to work, and after a few cold winters, I decided to get my license at age 26. Here I am 40 years old. No children, not married, have not had sex. I'm a late bloomer. But you know what? I accept that about myself. I'm fine. I'm content. I ask God to help me to be content in my life every single day. If I am so focused on what I do not have, I forget just how awesome I am. Not to be cocky or anything but I am a gift. I am the prize. Period!

LIFE/MENTAL HEALTH TIP(S):

I Thessalonians 4:3-4

It is God's will that you should be sanctified: that you should avoid sexual immorality; that each of you should learn to control your own body in a way that is holy and honorable.

5 Surprising Things That the Bible Says about Sex

The Bible is a book about God, about us, and about how God saves us through the person and work of Jesus Christ; therefore, it isn't terribly surprising to discover that the Bible has a great deal to say about sex. Human beings are sexual creatures – God made us male and female – therefore the story of creation, fall, and redemption is necessarily, at least in part, a story about human sexuality.

Parts of that story are relatively well known, but other parts can be quite unexpected – even shocking – to the first time Bible reader. Among the most surprising revelations would be the following:

1. It's good

In our contemporary culture, Christianity is generally portrayed as sexually repressive in the extreme. Christians are known for being opposed to gay sex, pre-marital sex, and extramarital sex and therefore the assumption is that Christians believe that sex is bad in and of itself – but nothing could be further from the truth!

The Bible says that the first husband and wife were: "both naked and were not ashamed" (Genesis 2:25 ESV).
Before the fall – before sin – sex was part of the created order. It was good – VERY GOOD – and was engaged in

103

freely, without inhibition of any kind by the man and the woman.

2. Husbands owe it to wives

Many historians think that the most surprising thing the Bible says about sex is found in 1 Corinthians 7:3-4:
The husband should give to his wife her conjugal rights, and likewise the wife to her husband. For the wife does not have authority over her own body, but the husband does. Likewise the husband does not have authority over his own body, but the wife does. (1 Corinthians 7:3–4 ESV)

The idea that sex was to be mutual and that the husband owed it to his wife – and that the wife had a right to claim it from the husband – was revolutionary! It was unprecedented! No one had ever said anything like this, anywhere else in the world.

3. Married couples should have it often

In addition to the goodness, generosity, and reciprocity mentioned above, the Scriptures also recommend a level of frequency that many modern Bible readers find quite surprising.

The Apostle Paul told his people:
Do not deprive one another, except perhaps by agreement for a limited time, that you may devote yourselves to prayer; but then come together again, so that Satan may not tempt you because of your lack of self-control. (1 Corinthians 7:5 ESV)

At most, married couples could set aside a few days for dedicated prayer and spiritual observance – only if both parties were in agreement – but then they must come together quickly lest they be tempted to sexual immorality. As in the Old Testament, so in the New, frequent marital intercourse is prescribed as a guard against a wandering eye and a lustful heart. The assumption is that if we drink deeply from our own cisterns we will be less tempted to draw from our neighbor's well. (Proverbs 5:15) There is great wisdom – and great joy – in following this inspired instruction.

4. It's not just about the kids
You don't have to read very far in the Bible to discover the connection between sexuality and procreation. In the very first chapter of the very first book it says:

So God created man in his own image, in the image of God he created him; male and female he created them. And God blessed them. And God said to them, "Be fruitful and multiply and fill the earth and subdue it. (Genesis 1:27–28 ESV)

That's true, but it isn't the end of the story – it isn't even the start of the story! In fact, the first thing that God says about a human being in the Book of Genesis is that: "It is not good that the man should be alone; I will make him a helper fit for him" (Genesis 2:18 ESV).

Sex in the Bible is first and foremost about intimate friendship. It is about cleaving to your God-given other. It is about becoming "one flesh". This Hebrew term implies more than, but not less than, physical union. It means almost becoming one person. Sex is about pursuing physical, emotional, sexual and ontological union. It is about submission, exploration, discovery, and delight.
Done right, under blessing, it often results in children, but it isn't ultimately for that. It is for the glory of God and the comfort of mankind. That's a subtle and yet very significant distinction.

5. It's not what makes you truly human
Despite all of what the Scriptures say in support and celebration of human sexuality, the Bible makes it very clear

that you can be fully and entirely human without ever having it.

Jesus never had it.
Nor did Jeremiah.
Or John the Baptist.
Or Elijah.
Or the Apostle Paul – at least for the better part of his life.

In fact, there are so many lifelong celibates in the Bible that some early Christians actually began to wonder if abstinence represented a sort of inside track to spiritual fulfillment. They wrote to Paul and asked him about that very thing. In response to their question, he spoke about marriage as a general rule (1 Corinthians 7:2); the need to be generous and reciprocal in the marriage bed (1 Corinthians 7:3-4) and the need for married couples to have sex on a regular and consistent basis (1 Corinthians 7:5). But then he said something very surprising to the modern reader. He said: I wish that all were as I myself am. But each has his own gift from God, one of one kind and one of another. (1 Corinthians 7:7 ESV)

Paul says that he wishes there were more lifelong celibates! He wishes there were more people who could do as he did – travelling the world, serving the Lord, feeding the flock and building up the people of God without worrying that he was neglecting his natural family. Paul says that if he had his way there would be MORE people like that – but each has his own gift from God. God gives to some the gift of marriage and to others, the gift of celibacy and Paul must submit to the Sovereign will of his Maker. What a surprising statement!

It means for starters that sex is natural for human beings, but not necessary. A person can live a full, blessed, rich, useful, meaningful, God-glorifying life without ever having sex with anyone. Sex is good but it's not ultimate. To many people in our culture, that would be the most surprising thing the Bible says about anything. The Bible says that marriage is good, sex is good, singleness is good and celibacy is good. They are all precious gifts given according to the wisdom and timing of the Lord for his glory and our everlasting good.

Reference:

https://www.google.com/amp/s/ca.thegospelcoalition.org/columns/ad-fontes/5-surprising-things-that-the-bible-says-about-sex/%3famp

EPILOGUE

I have learned through trials and triumphs to embrace my journey. I may not always understand my journey. I may not always agree with what's happening within my journey. I may not always make the best decisions while I am on my journey. However, I have NO REGRETS! I am entering year 41, filled with expectations for whatever my continued journey will bring. I am excited about my future, and I look forward to witnessing the fruition of every prophetic word spoken over my life. I am using this section of my book to share a few prophetic words spoken over my life. I will leave these words here as a reminder of God's promises for my life. I want to thank each of you for your support and for purchasing my book. If this book blessed you in any way, please pass it on to someone else. Again, thanks so much for your support!

Much Love,

Frenda

Prophetic Word
November 24, 2019
Prophet Arian Johnson

I heard the Lord say that, "You are on a long journey with Him, and it is literally a faith journey." And the Lord said, "What you are going to find is, at multiple points through this journey, the Lord is going to reward your faith in Him, and your willingness to step out, when there really was not much, but a desire, and a burden, and allow God to work, to plan out, to structure, and to put together." God is going to pull from different places, to bring into manifestation what you feel like God is calling you to. This is, for you, God moving you into what sometimes feels like passion, but it's really purpose. And it is much more expansive than you had even realized.

I see the Lord building through you a network that provides resources to underprivileged children. There's going to be resources for single mothers, and then, I am looking at educational resources, as a part of this overarching network. The Lord is going to staff you with resources. I feel like this has been a part of your request and your desire. "Okay God, I will do this, but I need the resources to do this." And the Lord has heard this, and He is about to grant it unto you, because your desire and your request for this has not been selfish. You're not requesting of yourself or even for selfish purpose.

It is a burden that God put in you to bring children out of, or to stop them, from experiencing what you experienced as a child. It's almost like, "I experienced this, and I don't want any other child to experience this. So, I am building this, as a resource, to bring them out of, to snatch them out of the grips of what I experienced."

And, this thing has so pleased God. You are about to walk into some of the best seasons of your life. You're about to walk into some of the most prosperous seasons....when I say, "Prosperous." I mean even beyond the money. You are going to find that while you felt like this season was going to be just about work, at expending energy in work. That is meant to be a part of it. But, this is really about God giving you your joy back. The Lord is going to do a thing with your joy in this season, you're going to find that working at that school had sapped your joy. God is getting ready to give it back to you.

He is getting ready to cause it to overflow, overflow, and overflow. And, this is a little bit strange, but there is a part of your grace that is for teenage men. I don't know. Who that is? I don't know why, but normally, you would think it would be men graced for men and women for women. But, I feel like God has called you to teenage men. God has put within you, this mother thing. And you are going to do for them, what their mothers did not do, and bring them into emotional health and emotional wholeness. And, the Lord's promise to you is, "If you will do this for me, I will make sure that your legacy will be intact."

There has been a fear from hell, that you would not be able to build legacy through family. But, the Lord says to you, "Daughter, that is not so. I will not allow you to help all the people, and their family, and their children come into legacy, and not do it for you." The Lord says, "Daughter, know that what I've been building on the inside of you is a woman of great faith, and a woman of mighty, mighty encounters with me."

There's also coming upon you a season of mentorship. God is getting ready to pour you out as a drink offering in this season. There is so much wisdom down on the inside of you. And I feel like, sometimes people look at your personality, and feel like you don't have much, but that that is not so. I have called you to be a well, a deep reservoir. And in this, the people are going to see the gift, and the grace of God, that is on the inside of you.

And the Lord says to you, "Daughter, know that I am even getting ready to cause you to come into great recompense." There are sacrifices that you have made for your sisters. That you have said, "Nobody else can do this." And put the burden upon you because you are the oldest. You sacrifice for them, and God is about to reward you. This is a symptom of recompense. And I feel like, because you are the oldest sister, and past times, made you feel like you have got to fill in the gaps for where your mother lacked. And the things that she could not do. And the Lord says to you, "I'm also going to reward you for doing that, because it was not necessarily your responsibility to do it. But in your selflessness, you put yourself out there for it. Prepare yourself for great days are ahead." And the Lord says to you, "You're about to see my wondrous and my mighty works, even though you."

Father, I thank you for this woman of God. And I decree and declare over her. Oh Father, your goodness, your peace, your favor, and your prosperity. I decree as your prophet; that she would know, and taste of your goodness. I decree in the name of Jesus, that you would release resources, from the North and the South, the East and the West. I thank you. There is no lack in her household. And everything that she needs, your hand would provide. Now Father, I rebuke the spirit of fear. And I thank you that it would not have any power over her. I release perfect love to cast out fear. I release perfect love to perfect her in you. In the name of Jesus, cause her heart to be subtle in the act. Your promises are still, yes, and amen. You have not changed your mind concerning her, but if you spoke it, you are going to do it. I thank you because it is so. It will not be otherwise. In Jesus name. Amen.

Prophetic Word
August 25, 2019
Prophet Jimmy Mitchell

What I began to hear the Lord say was, "Daughter, I have not been unjust to forget your labor of love." And the Lord says, "Daughter, your faithfulness and even your contentment in the season that you have been in, even as it pertained to your singlehood." The Lord says, "Daughter, know that you are on my heart as it pertains to your matrimony." And the Lord says, "Daughter, I'm going to arrange, I'm even going to cause the season to come, where I will cause the veil to even be lifted off of you." The Lord says, "Like Esther, I'm grooming you and I'm preparing you." And the Lord said, he has been very proud of how content you have been in your process and even in your journey. But the Lord says, "Daughter, like Sarah...I'm going to begin to open your womb." And God says, "You will know what it is even to conceive, even to have your own children." And God says, "Even to create legacy."

And God even says, "That I will place a burden upon you for adoption." The Lord says, "I'm even going to cause for you to create futures for those who don't have it, even for those that were not born into healthy families." The Lord says, "Daughter, I'm going to make sure that your legacy lives beyond you." But the Lord said, "It will not just be those that you adopt." But God says, "There will be children that will come from your loins." And the spirit of grace even says, "I'm even causing faith to arise in that place again." And God says, "Not even loss of expectation. I'm just causing your faith to come to a new level."

And the Lord had shown me, that Frenda, he's getting ready to prepare you for a season of ownership. The Lord says, "I'm going to bless you with a house." And God says, "Daughter, as you partner with what I'm doing, and as you partner with what I desire to do, even in the year of 2020, I'm going to blow your mind." The Lord says, "Daughter, you have not seen my hand yet." But the Lord says, "You are going to see me do things, it is going to be consecutively back to back to back." And the Lord says, "Daughter, even as you have postured yourself to be a fountain of wisdom." The Lord says, "I'm about to bring you into a season, not just of my wisdom but also my revelation." God says, "The revelation of what I desire to do in your life over the next 10 years." The Lord says, "I have desired to give you insight, even revelation as to what you are to do."

I see that the Lord is going to almost like play chess with you. The Lord is going to literally play chess with you. God's going to take you from one place to another place, to another place. And the Lord says, "It's going to almost seem like you're unstable." But the Lord said, "It's not instability because you hate instability." The Lord says, "It's going to be my hand." God says, "You are used to things being line upon line, precept upon precept." But the Lord says, "I'm trying to create another level of faith in you." So God says, "Partner with what I desire to do." I literally see the gift of faith coming alive in you. And the Lord says, "Daughter, there is a dormant gift for healing even in you." The Lord said, "There's a healing gift. It was not just for the mind, through your mouth." But the Lord says, "Through the laying on of the hands." The Lord says, "Daughter, I am going to prosper you."

And I even see where the Lord is getting ready to do a thing, with your salary. The Lord says, "There's going to come dramatic increase and there's going to come dramatic promotion." And God says, "I'm about to make room for you." I hear the scripture that says, I raise up one and I sit another down. The Lord said, he's about to remove wicked people, even out of the system. You have asked the Lord why he has kept you in the educational system. Why has he kept you in that arena? But the Lord says, "Because I have a place for you." And God's now making room for you. And God says, "You're going to end up where you had not anticipated." But the Lord said, "It is my plan and it is my desire." God says, "I will teach you and coach you along the way." The Lord says, "Just yield to me. Just comply and you're going to see great fruit and great harvest towards the middle of next year, you're going to see such a harvest come."

I literally feel like you've almost been feeling like a shift is coming. You just don't know what it is. But the Lord says, "Things are about to shift in your career." And God says, "Things are about to shift in your relational life." So God I bless her. And I thank you for what you're doing in Frenda's life. I pray that God, you give her grace and you give her courage even as you told Joshua, "Be strong and of good courage." And I thank you, father that she's going to give birth to natural children and I thank you, God, for grace to adopt. I thank you, God that the blessing of the Lord makes rich and adds no sorrow. And I thank you that Frenda is a crown. You've made her a crown, and I thank you that she will be a crown to her husband. I thank you, father. Even for a son. God, I thank you, father, for a son of promise. And I thank you that you're going to bless her and you're going to cause these things to come to pass in Jesus' name. Amen.

Prophetic Word
March 25, 2019
Dr. Matthew L. Stevenson III
All Nations Worship Assembly

Frenda, I declare and prophesy the favor of God on your life. I prophesy, and I declare that your season of frustration is over and that the spirit of God has not forgotten nor has He overlooked your years of investment in other people's visions and other people's programs. I declare and prophesy this time next year your life will be nothing like it is, and I declare that

God's reward to you is you will never have a regret. He is moving regret out of your life, and you will live as a rewarded woman. I prophesy that over you in the name of Jesus.

Prophetic Word
May 22, 2016
Dr. Matthew L. Stevenson III
All Nations Worship Assembly

You have allowed God to open up a conversation with you that you did not almost want to have with God. It was almost like in order to handle yourself, you closed up your heart. But I heard God say, "I am going to open your heart in such a way that you will see your decision for purity was not in vain." It has made you so angry that it seemed like your decision to live right before the Lord had no awards or benefits but Frenda, I tell you as God's prophet, He is going to reward you. He's going to reward you and He is going to deal with this thing in you…. I am telling you sweetheart it will be so that will have as many children as you want. Satan, I see you….. I see Satan playing "Great America" on the inside of you now (emotionally)…on rollercoasters and see-saws and it mainly happens at night time when he starts to bully you about that….I heard God say, I will not allow you to be mocked! You have given God an offering that most women would never give. God said, "Watch me show off on your behalf!" You will not have settle. You won't have to compromise. I prophecy that. God is going to send you someone that's going to fit your life and help you fulfill your ambitions. Hear this! God said, "The reason why a lot of your plans have been paused is because I have a partner that has the other half." God is going to bless you! He's going to bless you. Father give Frenda peace…complete peace…that there will be nothing broken or nothing missing. I hear the Lord say, "Because peace was stolen from you from years one to twenty, you we see in this season of your life there will be more peace than you've ever had, there will be nothing broken, there will be nothing missing and there will be nothing absent from your life." I heard God say, "Don't treat me like I am aloof because I am not a liar! I will reward you!"

ABOUT THE AUTHOR

Frenda Rodgers is the Director of A.C.C.E.S.S. Life, College, Career & Educational Signature Consulting; where she provides Life counseling, college and career exploration and development and academic coaching services. Frenda was employed as a high school counselor for Chicago Public Schools for 16 years. Frenda also serves as a Leader at All Nations Worship Assembly Chicago.

Frenda Rodgers holds a Bachelors in Psychology from Spelman College; a Masters in Social Work from the University of Illinois at Chicago; a Masters in School Counseling from Concordia University and a Masters in School Leadership from Concordia University. Frenda is currently working on a PhD in Human Services with a concentration in Social and Community Services at Capella University.

Made in the USA
Monee, IL
25 July 2020